*Rick, Kathy, Nicky, Barron
and Conrad Hilton*

Invite you to join them in celebrating

Paris Hilton's 21st Birthday

Wednesday, February 13th, 2002

*Light o'clock Cocktails
Nine o'clock Dinner
Ten Thirty 'til . . . Cake Celebration and Dancing*

*Studio 54
254 West 54th Street
(between Eighth Avenue & Broadway)*

*R.S.V.P. by February 11th to   Dressy/Funky
Kathy Hilton 212-555-5100   Cocktail Attire*

This invitation is strictly non-transferable

Confessions of an Heiress

Confessions of an Heiress

A Tongue-in-Chic Peek Behind the Pose

Paris Hilton with Merle Ginsberg

PHOTOGRAPHS BY

JEFF VESPA AND WIREIMAGE

A FIRESIDE BOOK

PUBLISHED BY SIMON & SCHUSTER

NEW YORK   LONDON   TORONTO   SYDNEY

FIRESIDE

Rockefeller Center

1230 Avenue of the Americas

New York, NY 10020

Fireside and colophon are registered trademarks

of Simon & Schuster, Inc.

For information regarding special discounts for bulk purchases, please contact Simon & Schuster

Special Sales at 1–800–456–6798 or business@simonandschuster.com

Designed by Charles Kreloff

Manufactured in the United States of America

10   9   8   7   6   5   4

Library of Congress Cataloging-in-Publication Data is available.

ISBN 0–7432–6664–1

I dedicate this book to

my late grandmothers,

Marilyn Hilton and

Kathy Richards.

Acknowledgments

I want to thank everyone in my family: my mom, Kathy, and dad, Rick Hilton; my sister, Nicky, and brothers, Barron and Conrad; and my grandfather Barron Hilton. And everyone in my extended work family: my managers, Jason Moore and Alissa Vradenburg, at Untitled Entertainment in Los Angeles; my favorite photographer, Jeff Vespa, and my favorite writer, Merle Ginsberg; my literary agent, Dan Strone, at Trident Media Group, and his assistant, Hilary Rubin; my editor, Trish Todd, at Touchstone Fireside, and all the people at Touchstone Fireside who worked so hard on this book; my UTA agents, Brett Hansen, Jim Berkus, and Alex Schaffel; WireImage's Andrea Collins and all the WireImage photographers for being so nice to me; Catherine Saxton; Eva Karloczy; Donald Trump; David Patrick Columbia; Wendy White; Joel Silver; Warner Bros.; Jon Murray and the memory of Mary Ellis Bunim of Bunim-Murray; Gail Berman at Fox; Gina Hoffman and Tracy Shaffer at PMK/HBH; all my lawyers at Ziffren Brittenham; my music attorney, Peter Lopez; Barbara (Jo Jo) Dellit; Brian Long; Wendy White; Henry Bouchekara; my dog, Tinkerbell, for being *such* a good model; and everyone who worked on the photo shoots for this book.

And everyone else who knows I love them—I'm just blanking on your names

—PH

Contents

Confessions of an Heiress

How to Be an Heiress

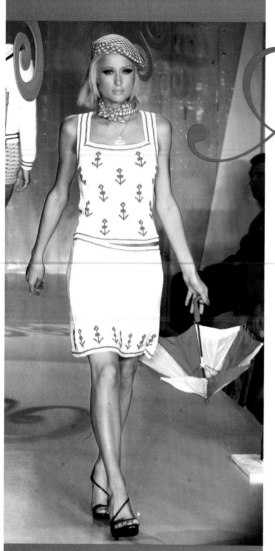

A lot of people seem to have the wrong idea about me. In fact, pretty much everything I read about myself is totally ridiculous. Newspapers and magazines write that I'm spoiled and privileged, and that all I do is dance on tabletops and party with my friends. They think I instantly became famous because I was born into a rich, well-known family, and everything has come so easily to me. They like to think *everything* they read about me in the tabloids is true. Well, you can't always believe what you read, right? So I've finally decided to give you a sneak peek into my very hyped life—so you can know the real me.

I haven't bothered to correct what's been written about me so far because, well, gossips believe whatever they want anyway. The people I care about know the real me. If I'm happy with who I am, what difference does it make?

And that's the bottom line for me. While the stuff printed about me over the last few years is amusing and makes me laugh, I've finally decided to let the world know: Okay, *I get it*. Everyone can have fun with my image because *I* like to have fun with it too. My friends know that while I like my lifestyle, I don't take it—or my media image—all *that* seriously. I do take my family seriously. I take my dog, Tinkerbell, seriously. I take my work seriously. But I don't take myself all that seriously.

Now, I have to confess to you: Despite what you've read, being a famous heiress is *not* that easy. It is, of course, fun and exciting, and it comes in handy for air travel. But look around you, and in the gossip columns: Not every heiress is famous. Or fun. There are a lot of boring heiresses out there. What a waste, I say! These are people who are so afraid of what other people might think or write about them, they don't take advantage of all the possibilities that being an heiress hands you on a silver platter. They think there's a pre-scribed way of "being an heiress" that you're supposed to conform to. It involves wearing white gloves, big hats, and pearls, having some dowdy debut or a coming-out party, and going to fancy, snobby all-girl colleges—boring, old-fashioned stuff like that.

I totally disagree. There is no sin worse in life than being boring—and nothing worse than letting other people tell you what to do. I was one of the few heiresses to walk the runway as a model. A lot of people thought that was shocking. Why did I do it? Was it a desperate cry for attention, like the papers said? Hardly. It's not like I need any more attention. Did I do it for money? Of course not. Modeling doesn't pay that well, anyway, unless you're Gisele or Cindy Crawford, or, like Patti Hansen, you get to marry a rock star. I did it because it was fun.

Well, suddenly, everyone got all freaked out. It seems modeling wasn't on the list of socially acceptable activities for heiresses. Then, a year later, every other socialite started walking the runway. Now you can't keep them *off* the run-way. Now there are model agents in New York and L.A. who specialize in getting socialites jobs as models. And if I hadn't pursued it, it might never have happened. I mean, if I didn't do it, who would have? By being brave—and channeling my "inner heiress"—I created a new opportunity for young heiresses.

That is what being an heiress means to me: being in charge. After all, if you have money and certain advantages,

"I take my dog, Tinkerbell, seriously. I take my work seriously. But I don't take myself all that seriously."

no one should be in charge of your life but you. Especially after the age of twenty-one. I'm twenty-three now, but in a lot of ways, I always took matters into my own hands. I knew I wanted to be a model, actress, and singer from a pretty young age, so I told my parents, and they could tell I was serious. In so many ways, being an heiress is really all in your head. If you follow your own plans and dreams and you don't let anyone talk you out of them, then you'll start to get the hang of being an heiress. It's all about feeling entitled, which seems, for some weird reason, to make a very big impression—a good one. And who's more empowered than an heiress? Heiresses are born with privileges. If you walk into a room and know you're the most exciting person in the room because . . . you are, *then* you're feeling like an heiress. All you need after that is a good handbag, a great pose, and very high heels, and you're on your way. (Long blond hair doesn't hurt, either.)

The best way for me to tell everyone how to act and feel like an heiress is by doing this book. First of all, the book parties will be really fun! But beyond that, I want to put it out there that if you can channel your own inner heiress, create your own image, and project an extreme sense of confidence—even if you don't really feel it every moment—people will treat you differently. Sure, heiresses are born with privileges. But if an heiress doesn't project natural-born superconfidence, no one is going to take her seriously or put her on the pedestal she deserves to be on. Put yourself on your own pedestal, and then everybody else will, too. Always act like you're on camera, and the spotlight's on you. Always behave like you are the center of attention. Always act like you're wearing an invisible crown. I do. And it's always worked for me.

And try adding a little attitude to your normal behavior. For instance, if you expect people to do things for you, they will. If you act like a doormat, no one will lift a finger for you. That does *not* mean you should *ever* be mean, or snobby. A true heiress is never mean to anyone—except a girl who steals her boyfriend. An heiress should be a little above it all, but sweet. She can afford to be kind because she's well bred and never in a hurry. And she shouldn't go around spilling her guts to everyone. Have some secrets, I say. Secrets are very important assets if you're going to be an heiress.

Even if you have no secrets—and everyone does—you've got to make people think that you do. If people read a few tidbits about you in *Vanity Fair* or on "Page Six," they instantly want to know more. They will want to know *everything* about you. If there's one thing I've learned, it's this: People *need* to believe your life is better than theirs.

After all, everyone needs a fantasy. Okay, maybe I don't,

PARIS HEIRESS TIP

I love tiaras. They're so cute. I like to wear them to my birthday parties. Trust me, people act differently toward you when you've got jewelry on your head. Especially when they suspect it might be real.

but most rich people want something they can't have. If they have one Rolls-Royce, they fantasize about having two. If they have a closet full of Chanel, they want a closet full of Gucci.

I'm a fantasy to a lot of people. They *want* to think that I have more fun than they do, have fewer problems, wake up looking great, go to sleep looking great, can buy and eat anything in the world I want, and get any hot guy I want. They think I'm "Paris Barbie." (I take that as a compliment. Barbie is my total fashion icon!) No one wants to think that I have a normal life or problems. They prefer to imagine someone has the Perfect Life, and I guess mine seems like that to a lot of people. I've only been me, so I can't tell if my life is perfect or not.

The way I keep people wondering about me is to smile all the time and say as little as possible. Smile beautifully, smile big, smile confidently, and everyone thinks you've got all kinds of secret things going on. And that keeps them wanting more. And when they want more, you are automatically interesting. If you give too much away, no one needs to know anything else. You've given it all away—and for free. And if you do that, well, you're never going to have any money. Or make any money. It's what they call "supply and demand."

So, while I'm going to reveal some of my secrets here, don't get your hopes up *too* high. I'll never reveal ALL of them. How tacky would that be? An heiress never reveals how much money she's worth, or her family's worth. An heiress hardly ever refers to money, period. An heiress never reveals how many guys she's dated, or . . . whatever. There are definitely a number of things an heiress won't talk about. You can imagine what they are. There's a big difference between being fun and provocative and being totally over-the-top and gross. An heiress knows how to tread that fine line—in stilettos.

I've noticed that my girlfriends want to tell their friends everything. They need to talk about every tight T-shirt they buy, every carbohydrate they eat, every insecurity they have, every single thing a guy says to them. These girls have no secrets. So no one needs to talk behind their backs. They've spilled it all. I don't do that.

Rule Number One: Heiresses aren't needy. If an heiress is feeling a little insecure, she should go shopping. And if she still doesn't feel any better, she should go to Paris. Or Saint-Tropez. For the weekend, if necessary. Because there's always another fun place to visit, another set of fun people, another cute outfit waiting to be snapped up. There's no reason for an heiress to ever EVER be bored.

Rule Number Two: An heiress should never be too serious. Being too serious is very dull, and is a sign you have no imagination or personality. No one really wants to hang out with anyone too serious. An heiress is so confident—and why shouldn't she be?—that she should always be able to make fun of herself. First of all, if you make fun of yourself, no one gets upset when you make fun of other people. And if you make fun of yourself first, no one gets the urge to do it behind your back. You've  taken all the power away from them—AND made them laugh. It's a double whammy.

Here are my fail-safe instructions on how to be an heiress and live like you have a privileged life—and I *am* serious about them. Most of them, anyway.

My Instructions on How to Be an Heiress

1 *B*E BORN INTO THE RIGHT FAMILY. Choose your chromosomes wisely. This may seem like ludicrous advice, but actually it isn't. If an heiress is in control of everything, why shouldn't she be in control of who she's born to? You know how everyone always says there are no accidents? Well, I believe you choose who you're born to. And if you do have the misfortune of being born into the wrong family, remember: No one has to know. Airing family laundry is definitely a big no-no for an heiress. You can always reinvent yourself and your lineage if you have to. Half of Park Avenue and Bel Air have. Lineage can be a state of mind.

2 *H*AVE A GREAT NAME. If you are going to be an heiress, you can't have a normal name, unless you're British. All British people have plain names, and that works pretty well over there. But in America, you've got to have a name that stands out. I love my name. Paris is my favorite city. And *Paris* without the *P* is "heiress," isn't it? In sixth grade, people would make fun of me and call me "France" or "London." Well, I'm going to name my own daughter Paris! An heiress needs to have a glamorous—or a really cute—name. My sister Nicky's name is cute. An heiress's dog also needs to have a cute name. My teacup Chihuahua is named Tinkerbell, so she acts like a Tinkerbell. If you have a cute name, you will act cute. If you have a glam name, you will act glam. It's that simple. Future moms should make a note of that.

3 *H*AVE ABSOLUTELY FLAWLESS SKIN, but don't fret over it. Pile makeup on and never, ever have a breakout. Perfect skin is a birthright, and it means you can never really take a bad photograph. No amount of junk food or Coca-Cola can change your skin. And if, God forbid, it does, have a great makeup artist standing by. It can't hurt.

4 *E*AT ONLY FAST FOOD OR THE MOST FABULOUS FOOD. Greasy chips or perfect crab cakes. Cotton candy or caviar. Fast food or fois gras. French fries or black-pepper shrimp from the Ivy in L.A. Cheesy junk or expensive cheese. Being an heiress is all about extremes.

5 *D*EVELOP A WAY OF ENTERING A ROOM THAT LOOKS ROYAL AND REGAL BUT NOT SNOBBY. Learn how to pose in an onslaught of flashing lights without blinking. (Note to celebrities: You can always improve.) Always know your best angle—for your body and your face—and work it. Study your own pictures and you'll figure it out.

6 *N*EVER, EVER WAKE UP BEFORE TEN; NEVER GO TO BED BEFORE THREE. Normal hours are for normal people. You never want to be normal. Anyone can be normal. How boring. I'm yawning.

7 *A*LWAYS TELL EVERYONE WHAT THEY WANT TO HEAR. Then do what you want. That way, no one ever gets mad at you. They get very confused, then blame it on themselves. If anyone confronts you, smile sweetly and act coyly. Particularly with guys. And bosses. Try not to have bosses if you can avoid them. Or have your manager deal with them.

8 *N*EVER HAVE ONLY ONE CELL PHONE WHEN YOU CAN HAVE MANY. Lose one all the time. That way, if you haven't called someone back, you can blame it on the lost phone. It's very important to get a new model the minute it comes out. Nokias, Ericksons, Motorolas—those are the coolest. Always have at least two numbers: a friend line and a business line. If I feel like avoiding a call, I answer my phone in a phony British accent and say, "Hello, Paris Hilton's line," or something like that. I do that if I'm expecting a call from a guy I've changed my mind about and I don't want to have dinner with him anymore. Every woman has the right to change her mind from time to time; therefore heiresses have *more* of a right.

10 *D*ON'T WEAR A DRESS THAT'S IN ALL THE MAGAZINES. That's for girls with no imag ination who just buy what magazines tell them to buy. Look for the cool, unusual dress that no one else has the nerve to wear. Dare to be different. Dare to wear color and prints. All the boring New York socialite girls wear black. Do you ever see a girl in a magazine wearing black? I don't think so. Don't run out and buy the bag of the moment or the dress of the moment. I like expen sive things, but I like cheap things, too. I like anything that's cute and makes me happy. I haven't met too many clothes I didn't like—except black clothes.

11 *I*F YOU'RE HAPPY, WEAR PINK. If you're depressed, wear black. Black is for peo ple who don't want to have fun with clothes and who are always hiding—in other words, depressed. No one with a truly great body wears black, trust me.

9 *N*EVER WEAR THE SAME THING TWICE. This is particularly important if you're going to be photographed a lot, which I am. If you double up, people will think you have only one outfit—and that's annoying. And untrue.

And if you really want to stand out and be confident, wear white.

12 *MAKE PLANS, PLANS, AND MORE PLANS.* Invite everyone you know to come along. If there aren't enough hours in the day, don't worry, there will be. You live in a different time zone: Heiress Time.

13 *ACT DITZY. LOSE THINGS.* It throws people off and makes them think you're "adorable," and less together than you really are.

14 *IF ALL ELSE FAILS, ACT BORED.* Not boring. There's a huge difference.

15 *PUBLIC DISPLAYS OF AFFECTION ARE OKAY,* in limited amounts, but only with your serious boyfriend, because that's exactly what someone with a famous family name is NOT supposed to do. It makes other boys think you're dangerous, so they will all want you, too. Guys like women they're a little afraid of. No, make that *a lot* afraid of.

16 *ALWAYS HAVE A VERY BIG BODYGUARD.* It intimidates guys. If a guy does have the nerve to approach you when your bodyguard is around, you know he's got to be pretty fearless.

17 *ALWAYS HAVE A TAN.* It looks like you've been in an exotic (i.e., expensive) place. It can never look fake, even if it is. Get the spray-on tan, so it doesn't get all over your clothes.

18 CHANGE YOUR HAIRSTYLE ALL THE TIME. Everyone expects you to have the same hairstyle in every photo, and only dull people do that. Tell everyone you're wearing hair extensions even if you aren't, because they don't expect you to tell them.

19 NEVER DRINK DIET SODA. It shows yo have no nerve. Only drink real colas caffeine-packed energy drinks, or Vitamin Water. Hat champagne, because that's what everyone expects yo to love. Energy drinks are the best party drinks. Yo never get tired. You never have a hangover. And yo can make fun of all the loaded people who thin they're clever but are really acting stupid.

20 FEAR NOTHING—except insects. An sweaty guys who insist on kissing yo when they come up to say hello. There's nothin worse than a sweaty guy who kisses you on bot cheeks. Once is bad enough, but to have to go throug it twice is really two times too much.

21 NEVER BE PREDICTABLE. Always surpris people. That way, they will never ge tired of you.

22 IF THE MEDIA PLAYS WITH YOU, WEL PLAY WITH THEM. I went on *Saturda Night Live* soon after my name was in the headline every day for something I wasn't too proud of, an which had really upset my family. On "Weeken Update" with Jimmy Fallon, the script had him askin me, "Is it hard to get a room in the Paris Hilton? Is roomy?" and he wanted to cut it. But I wouldn't l him. No way. That was the funniest line. And I got th upper hand with the media the moment he said it o national TV. That's when it all clicked and thing started to change. People knew I could laugh a myself, and that one bad incident was not going t make me lock myself in my room.

23 LAST BUT NOT LEAST: MAKE FUN OF YOURSELF. NEVER TAKE YOUR-
SELF, OR RULES, TOO SERIOUSLY (see all above rules).

My List of Twelve Things an Heiress Would Never Do:

1. Be mean to animals.

2. Have roots in her hair. Or at least, ever let anyone see them. It's just not cool. It's ugly and unnecessary. If you're busy, get the colorist to come to your house.

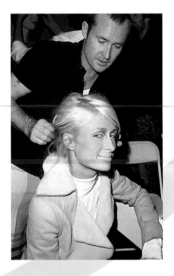

3. Go out the night after the Oscars.

4. Go out when it's raining, unless you have a Gucci umbrella.

5. Talk about money. It's boring, and only agents, lawyers, and managers should ever talk about money.

6. Go on the Atkins diet. Or the South Beach diet. Even if you are in South Beach. Especially if you are in South Beach. If you are in South Beach, eat more.

7. Eat caviar all the time. It's just what people expect. Caviar is for wanna-bes.

8. Carry your own luggage.

9. Spend the summer in New York. Or the winter in the Hamptons.

10. Stand in line for a movie. It's all about private screenings.

11. Wear an outfit another girl has been photographed in.

12. Listen to anyone else's rules for behavior—except MINE!

Three Things Most People Think Heiresses Shouldn't Do, But I Think They Should:

1. Go out with broke guys. Money doesn't matter if they're nice enough.

2. Dance with no self-consciousness. You only live once.

3. Accept free stuff. If people want to give it to me, why shouldn't I take it? I love it!

My Other Half

My Sister, Nicky

My sister, Nicky, is three years younger than I am, but we were raised like twins. We look a lot alike; my mom, Kathy, always dressed us alike; and since our two baby brothers (Barron and Conrad) are so much younger, Nicky and I grew up together. We always felt like we were the same age. We bonded over animals, which we both love, dolls, clothes, living in Los Angeles and the Waldorf-Astoria in New York, and the fact that we knew we were special and different. We were like a couple of cute blond Eloises running around the Plaza, except it was the Waldorf Towers, and it wasn't fiction.

I remember getting really excited when I found out my mom was pregnant. I was three, an only child, and I hoped it would be a girl. I was never jealous of Nicky after she was born. I was happy to have someone close. So many of my friends were only children, and many of them had divorced parents—so I definitely knew how lucky I was to have a sister and both parents around all the time.

We were a really close family, and that hasn't changed. I know it's unusual these days, and I definitely appreciate it and don't take it for granted. Even though Nicky is a little quieter than I am, and probably more serious, we've always had fun together and trusted each other in a world where it can be really hard to trust people. I don't know what I'd do without my sis-

ter. If it wasn't for her, I would have grown up pretty lonely. Instead, I *always* had a best friend. That's probably why I always feel confident. She made me feel even luckier than I already was.

Even when we fight, which, of course, we do occasionally, we're still super-close. All sisters fight, right? That's probably the only way Nicky and I are normal. When we were little, we'd fight over silly stuff—like if I would swear, she'd tell my mom. That made me so mad. I had to teach her not to tell. I would pull her aside and explain that it was us against them, that we two girls were a team. What's that line about divide and conquer . . . or something? Anyway, after that, she figured it out—we had to stay loyal to each other. Generally, we fight less than most sisters.

In fact, we've lived together in Hollywood for the last few years, since she was eighteen. We have a lot of the same friends; some different ones, of course, but our worlds mostly overlap when it comes to work. We're very into creating things now, and we've become pretty business-minded. We like performing. Nicky's doing some television hosting; during this year's Golden Globes and Academy Awards, she was on the red carpet for E! She has her own handbag line, which does particularly well in Japan—Nicky's are the best-selling handbags in Japan; the Japanese love us. We go there every couple of months to do promotion and photo shoots.

One of my favorite things to do with Nicky is to go with her to Japan. There's amazing shopping, it's fun, and the people are all really sweet. We have a ton of fans over there. Nicky and I have to wear black wigs, and we can't even walk next to each other! There's a shopping center in Tokyo we love to go to, but we have to split up so we're not followed by hordes of people. I start on the top floor, she starts on the bottom, and we meet in the middle. Even with wigs on, if we're together, they know it's us. We got caught in the corner of a

store once, and it was insane. People were screaming and acting like maniacs when they saw us! Which is crazy, because the Japanese are mostly so polite and friendly.

Yes, we're the Hilton Sisters, always talked about together in one breath. A sister act. Anything that happens to me happens to her. However, now that I've done *The Simple Life* and Nicky has dyed her hair, people don't associate us with each other as much as they used to. I love her dark hair. It looks amazing on her. Of course, it made everyone say that she wanted to separate herself from me, but I know that she just wanted to try something different. She's got beautiful blue eyes, so dark hair looks great on her. She'd been talking about dyeing it brown for so long, and she finally did it. And I think it looks better on her than blond. I would never do it, unless it was for a movie and I had to. I love being blond. It's a big part of my identity. But then, so is Nicky. And I love that.

My Earliest Memories of Nicky

I remember living in Bel Air when Nicky and I were three and six, and we used to fly down the driveways on Rollerblades. We didn't know how to stop, so we'd go crashing into anything. We were pretty animated. Mom had this high bed and we'd climb on top of it and jump off. We definitely liked to perform, too. Nicole Richie's dad, Lionel, had a jukebox, and we would lip-synch the songs it played. Nicky, Nicole, and I would put makeup on and dance to Tina Turner, Whitney Houston, Madonna, and Prince. We would get all decked out in my mom's clothes and jewelry, then we'd do the show at parties for our parents. It was pretty cute!

Nicky and I always went to the same schools. My mom made sure we were always together, and we continued to dress alike into our early teens. I think my mom thought it would give us more confidence, and she was right. She always bought two sizes of the same outfit if she liked it, so we wouldn't get jealous of each other's clothes.

In school, I loved art class and Nicky loved writing, so we'd help each other with homework. We never, ever liked the same guy. Some sisters do, but we never did, luckily. That would be a total drag. We like different types of guys. Nicky and I have opposite taste.

I remember this funny story from when we were about five and eight: Nicky's god-father, Parviz, was my dad's best friend. He would always give her a hundred dollars on her birthday. (Where was *my* hundred dollars?) I soon realized that if I got a toy that Nicky wanted, I could sell it to her for the hundred dollars! She was sooo young and looked up to me, so she went along with it. Then I'd buy another toy for myself and keep her money. I have to admit, I feel bad about that now.

Nicky and I got the shopping bug pretty early. I remember we would put a table in front of our bedroom door and make a little shop. We'd pretend to sell stuff to our parents and their friends, and we'd want real money! I guess that was my first memorable experience with stores and shopping. It sure wasn't the last.

"The only person who really knows me is Nicky."

When we were on the verge of becoming teenagers, Nicky and I started getting into trouble. Not big-time trouble, just your normal kid stuff, though we always thought it was a big deal when it happened. Like a lot of our friends, we'd make prank phone calls, leave messages for dogs on answering machines, and silly stuff like that. Then we'd play "school," and I'd always get to be the teacher because I'm the oldest of all the cousins. Once, I remember, I made the "class" say the Pledge of Allegiance—which would have been cute, except I put it through our house's P.A. system and it went all over the house, and kind of surprised everybody. And when Nicky and I would play that we were royalty, I'd always be the queen, and I'd make her be the princess. But it seems to me now that all older sisters do stuff like that. Age is much more obvious when you're kids.

Then, when we were a little older and lived in the Waldorf, we once dressed up and snuck into a ball—no one knew it was us. We'd dance around and act all cute, and it didn't occur to anyone to throw us out. I think the hotel staff was afraid of us, even though we were just children.

All Grown Up Together

When Nicky was eighteen, she wanted to leave New York and move to L.A. I was living in Hollywood, and I had just broken up with my then-boyfriend. I didn't want to be by myself in Hollywood Hills, and because I travel a lot, I wanted someone to watch my animals. So I convinced Nicky to move in with me. It's so nice to have her here, to have someone to talk to and watch a movie with. She's the perfect roommate because I can just be myself—and I can trust her. You can't trust anyone the way you can trust a family member. Plus, it's always fun to make an entrance at a party with Nicky. She always tells me the truth about which outfit looks best. And not many people know this, but my sister is one of the funniest people you'll ever meet.

Even though we're alike in so many ways, we're different in one crucial aspect: She's better at shopping than I am. Hard to believe, I know! But I get bored fast, and I wear more costumey clothes—wild, crazy, funky stuff from all kinds of shops on Melrose or downtown Manhattan. Nicky's more sophisticated—she only wears high-fashion designers, and she prefers bigger, fancier stores. Nicky is one of the best-dressed women I know. At the age of fifteen, she was voted by *Vogue* one of the best-dressed women in the world! And lately, I find myself dressing more and more like her. However, neither of us mind if we happen to like the same outfit, and each of us will get one. We don't really share clothes because, while she trusts me with a lot of things, she doesn't trust me not to ruin her outfits! That might seem a little excessive, but it does prevent fights.

Nicky's a little more strict and uptight with her friends than I am, and she's definitely shier. I'm nice to everybody, which attracts a lot of people. Nicky doesn't like to be around a ton of people, and she doesn't like all of my friends. That's okay. I'm always happy to be in the eye of the storm, but I get that she's not. It's not for everybody. But my sister rocks, and I never have as much fun with anyone as I have with her.

Luckily, as I said, we've never liked the same guy, so she's the one girl I've always trusted with my boyfriends, no matter what. Our bond is stronger than any bond either of us could ever have with a guy.

People are always asking me what kind of advice I give Nicky about guys, because I'm older and have always had boyfriends. Well, Nicky's so smart, I don't have to give her much advice. But I did tell her that guys are only going to want what they can't have. No one wants the beaten-up fake Prada purse on Canal Street. Everyone wants the brand-new colorful Louis Vuitton that no one can get. Guys don't want the girl who's been around the block. I think girls are confused when they're sixteen. They'll hook up with guys and think that's the way to get them. The girls need to learn to hold out. Everyone thinks I've been with so many guys, but that's just because every time I'm seen with a guy, everyone thinks I've "been" with him. It's so completely untrue, but it's too boring to have to deny it all the time. I just have a lot of guy friends. People can think what they want. The only person who really knows me is Nicky. We'll always be there for each other. She's always proud of me, in the good times and the rough. And that's a wonderful thing to know and to have grown up with.

So if you really want to act like an heiress, try to get a good-looking sibling you can trust. That way, you'll never have to go shopping alone, and you'll always have somebody you can trust.

Fashion and Beauty

What, When, Wear, and How Low Can I Go?

J think fashion is in my blood. When Nicky and I were little girls, there was nothing we loved to do more than get dressed up. We would do little modeling shows at home, using our mom's clothes, jewelry, and makeup. Our mom has always inspired our style. When we were little, we'd look at her fashion magazines and try to pose like the models. Then we'd look at each other in the mirror and laugh. But I think we knew we weren't totally fooling around.

I guess I started to think seriously about modeling when I was around fifteen. I was pretty flat-chested, so what else was I going to do? Most of the supermodels are small, except for a few, who probably won't age well. I knew I had to turn being flat into a plus. I was so embarrassed to be flat-chested that I wore padded bras until I was seventeen. Now I don't care. I'm happy to be small, because I look good in clothes. But, boy, back then I was really insecure.

At sixteen, I asked my mother if I could model in New York. Modeling agents had approached me, and designers and photographers asked me to model all the time. I would get really dressed up and go to events, and my picture started running in lots of different places. But my mom just wouldn't let me. She was worried about what might happen to a young girl who began modeling in New York. So I didn't start doing it professionally until I turned seventeen, and even then I didn't do it full-time—it was more for fun.

Fashion Shows

I think designers were a little nervous about booking me at first because they thought of me more as a socialite than a model. But who says you can't be both? I was very selective about which shows I was in.

But this is something an heiress inherently knows: Always be more important than your clothes. Even on a runway. There are a lot of socialites who still don't get this concept. Supposedly, Marilyn Monroe said that if someone complimented her dress instead of her, she'd get insulted. That's why I don't always wear designer clothes. I don't want my clothes to get more attention than I do. How can you brand yourself if you're in somebody else's label?

I've modeled for a number of designers I like, including Alvin Valley. I love the pants he makes. He uses a hairdresser, Ricardo, who did this hairstyle for me that was like a Gwen Stefani mohawk—I loved that 'do. That was one of my all-time favorites, and I love looking at the pictures from that show. For Valley's show, I wore these cool bandeau tops, something you can't do if your boobs are too big. I also did the Joey and T show in L.A., and Taryn Manning and Jamie Presley were in it as well. Aimee Osbourne was also in that show, so Sharon and Ozzy were in the audience.

I go to lots of fashion shows, too. My favorite in Paris and Milan is Versace, both couture and ready-to-wear. I love Donatella's clothes; she always gives Nicky and me the most beautiful dresses to wear to her shows and after-parties. And she has the coolest crowd. I love Tommy Hilfiger's shows; there are always hot guys modeling his men's collections. Hey, guys go to fashion shows to ogle girl models, why can't I go to look at boy models? Anyway, Tommy's really nice, and I love his look. It's preppy in a very cool way. I like Catherine Malandrino's shows, too. She did a

PARIS HEIRESS TIP

Fashion magazines can help bring out your inner heiress. Used to be, their pages were filled with gorgeous models in gorgeous clothes. But who is in the front row of all those fashion shows? And who do you think can afford those clothes? Heiresses, of course. Well, the magazines finally figured that out. Now all the fashion magazines feature socialites and heiresses almost as much as celebrities and models. Hint: Not all those socialites and heiresses are the real deal; they just know how to act the part. And they can often get store discounts—if they've got the nerve to ask for them.

cool American-flag theme a few years back. Diane von Furstenberg's collections are amazing. Her dresses are beautiful; I must own at least fifty. She always has the most exciting people in her front row, and she totally gets it about socialites and heiresses. And I've been in Heatherette's shows, which are so much fun. I'm their muse, which, of course, I love. Their clothes are cool, funky, and crazy—all about clubbing, since they're former N.Y. club kids! I love really theatrical shows.

But I don't know if I could handle being a full-time model. After all, you have to keep a straight face, and I LOVE to smile. I show up with fast food and the models get upset; they wish they could eat it.

Anyway, the audience is often a lot more interesting than what's on the runway. What's the point of going to a fashion show and getting all dressed up if you can't people-watch? Some of the best action happens off the runway, between the socialites, the editors, and the guys who hit on the models. There's so much gossip flying around at fashion shows, it makes my head spin.

My Crowning Glory

Here's one of my major secrets revealed: I have curly hair. I get it blown straight all the time so no one has to know. I would look like Shirley Temple if I didn't blow it out. When I was a child, it wasn't curly. But I can't get it professionally straightened because it would fry my hair. So I have to go to the salon a few times a week. Oh well, that's just how it turned out. Nicky's hair is naturally straight—that makes me insane, too.

I love changing my hairdo almost more than I love changing clothes. There's a reason you rarely see my hair look the same way twice: I get creative. I love to look different, and changing my hairstyle is a great way to accomplish that. I go to lots of different salons in Beverly Hills and New York, because getting my hair done by different stylists is a luxury I never deny myself. (There are others, of course, but this is the hair section.)

I go from a choppy bob to long hair, then back again, all the time. I love long hair, but hair extensions do hurt. Chris McMillan in L.A. cuts my hair—he's the only one I trust to chop it. He does have a huge waiting list, but, he manages to fit me into his busy schedule. When I want an amazing 'do or a supersexy cut, I will also go to Guy Riggio at Sally Hershberger for John Frieda salon in L.A. Guy is a genius with hair. I also like Prive, Jose Eber, Cristophe, or Frédéric Fekkai in New York or L.A. Yukimi Kakumo Smith of the Kenneth Salon in the Waldorf-Astoria has been my hairstylist for years and gives the best haircut and blow-dry in New York. A true heiress always has many hair salons at her disposal. One is definitely not enough. After all, every hairdresser will have a different vision of you.

As for color, well, blondes have more fun! And I'm living

proof. We stand out more. My color is done mostly by Michael Boychuck, the head colorist and director of the Canyon Ranch Salon at the Venetian Hotel in Las Vegas. He flies to L.A. for me, and he brings his head hair-extension person, Antonia Ravenda-Stilianessis. They know how to do my hair so that I'll love it.

In New York, I go to Parveen Klein at John Barrett, which is located on the top floor of Bergdorf Goodman. I love that the salon is at Bergdorf's, and Parveen is the best with blond shades. (They didn't call that book *Bergdorf Blondes* for nothing.) She's the one who dyed Nicky's hair brown, and look how great she looks. I like to put hot-pink pieces in my hair, too. Parveen can do anything.

Yes, it's hard to believe, but I do sometimes have bad-hair days! If I'm tired of my hair and I don't have a lot of time, I'll wear a hat. A hat changes your look really fast, and you definitely get noticed. Hats are cute. I like berets; they add a little international flair.

I find hair salons to be so relaxing. If all else fails, and you aren't getting your minimum daily attention requirement, a hairdresser can not only fill in nicely for a boyfriend, but is also a great person to gossip with. He or she is being paid to be all about you. And going to a stylist is tons better than going to a therapist. You get to talk while someone plays with your hair. It feels good.

I don't really like waiting or sitting around, though. Who does? For photo shoots, styling can take four hours or more if they do hot rollers and teasing. To kill time, I'll read magazines or scripts, cruise the Internet, browse eBay, or look for the latest pics on WireImage.

My Beauty Secrets

MAKEUP

My favorite lip gloss is Prrr by MAC. It's a cute, shiny light pink, and because it's inexpensive, you can buy tons of it and carry one in every handbag.

I'm partial to the smoky-eye-and-light-lip look, which I don't stray from very often. If it was okay for Brigitte Bardot, it's okay for me. I love black eyeliner and fake eyelashes—the individual ones. That's my look: bronze skin, pink lips, blond hair. While it's fun to change your hairstyle, your face is your trademark. Not only that, heiresses are by definition a little subtle. Have you ever noticed that no one who grew up rich wears a lot of makeup? It's just not classy. Red lipstick makes me look like a clown. And if you're going to wear colorful clothes, you've got to tone down the makeup. Besides, guys don't like girls who wear a lot of makeup. It just gets on their clothes.

I try to have my makeup done by a professional when I go out because it makes such a difference. It looks better on camera and lasts much longer. You can even sleep in it, and it won't look that bad in the morning. And yes, you can sleep in fake eyelashes—they will still be there when you wake up. Heiresses and divas know that trick.

SKIN CARE

When it comes to keeping a year-round Saint-Tropez-looking tan, Mystic Tan is key. It gives you a great glow that you can't get from bronzer. I'm over tanning beds, because I really don't want to get skin cancer. By the way, have you ever seen a pale heiress? I think not. Even in New York in February. Especially in New York in February.

I have to admit, I'm really bad about washing my face and using skin products. A lot of my friends have these really strict beauty regimens, but I'm pretty lazy about that stuff. It should all look like it comes naturally for true heiresses. I've actually found that sleeping in makeup can be good for my skin. It makes it look kind of dewy. And then I don't have to do too much in the morning.

Of course, I live in fear of pimples. Who doesn't? Now, if you do break out, or have circles under your eyes after a late night, a great makeup artist can fix it in a second. It's worth paying a lot of money for. And never, ever point out your pimples or circles to anybody—certainly not a guy, and not even to a close girlfriend. Chances are they won't notice when the rest of you is so fabulous.

Even Heiresses Have Flaws

Okay, I admit it—I desperately hate one thing about my body: I have size 11 feet. I can't believe people care what shoe size I wear! I mean, I'm not a guy, so it doesn't mean anything! Yeah, it sucks. But really, I don't even care anymore. It sucks because in stores I see all these supercute shoes like Guccis, YSLs, and Manolos. And when they're brought out in my size, they look like clown shoes on me! I can't wear flats because my feet are too long. At least high heels shrink how long my feet look. But forget about ever seeing me in ballet slippers or tennis shoes: I'd look like I was wearing canoes!

I do, however, love Ugg-style fuzzy-lined boots, especially the light pink and blue ones with pom-poms or sequins that Steve Madden makes. I started wearing them at the Sundance Film Festival because there's a lot of snow in Park City, and now I wear them with my velour sweat suits all the time. At least Ugg-like boots are so wide that no one can tell the size of

THE PARIS DIET

I know this diet is not for everybody, and I'm not even sure you should try it at home. But it works for me. And I think there's some Dr. Atkins–type stuff in here. Wasn't he all about eating fat?

• Don't be afraid to eat fast food as often as you can. Always order the largest portion of French fries. Otherwise, you'll just want more.

• Eat pasta as often as you can. I cook the best lasagna at home. Who says heiresses shouldn't know how to cook? Just because you grew up with a staff doesn't mean you shouldn't be able to surprise the pants off your friends by cooking a great dinner once in a while.

• Eat sushi, because the coolest and best-looking people eat sushi.

• Eat as much chocolate as you can. Chocolate seems sinful, and therefore makes you happy.

• Eat popcorn at night. In fact, eat all carbs at night. In fact, ONLY eat carbs at night. Never listen to what diet doctors tell you.

• If you're in L.A., eat at Johnny Rockets or In-N-Out Burger as often as you can.

• Never take diet pills!

• Do what you want. Life is too short not to enjoy it. Just keep busy, go out at night, and dance away the calories!!

my feet in them. Plus, they look really cute when you tuck your pants into them. So my advice to girls with big feet like mine: Wear very high heels, or Ugg-style boots.

Try to keep your shoe size out of the papers. If you can't, then just get over it. Fast.

How to Shop Like an Heiress

Contrary to what you might think, I'm not a snob about shopping. Sure, I like Barneys, but I also like a lot of funky small stores in L.A. and New York too. I'm loving the Tracy Feith store on Melrose. Tracey Ross's store in the Sunset Plaza is another one of my favorites. And I live for the T-shirts at Kitson on Robertson in L.A. It's the best place to buy gifts for birthdays, et cetera. I don't need all designer clothes, except for premieres and events. And usually designers just lend me their clothes, because once I'm photographed in them, I can't ever wear them again. So what's the use of owning them? I'd just wind up giving them to a friend. Or to charity. That's the true heiress thing to do.

I never let anyone in a store tell me

what looks good on me. To me, it's important for a person to figure out her own sense of style, rather than have it imposed on her. By the age of eighteen, every girl needs to know what her style is and what looks good on her. Most salespeople just want to make money off you and will sell you anything. They'll talk you out of jeans and into a gown in a heartbeat. Not only that—who wants to dress like them? I make sure I go shopping with Nicky, a stylist, or by myself. Shopping with your boyfriend is a good idea, too, because he'll communicate how he likes you to look by smiling and staring at you; guys aren't too good at telling you that in words, though. They don't know how to talk about clothes. If they do, well, you should probably make him your boyfriend in about two seconds.

And I also like to buy things off photo shoots, because stylists bring hard-to-find stuff I like. Lately, I've been feeling like I want to change my look, to all really high fashion. Or couture. To me, that means "lady" in public and fun in private.

"Always be more important than your clothes."

My Wardrobe Dos and Don'ts

• IF YOU WEAR JEANS, WEAR THEM REALLY, REALLY LOW-WAISTED. I know everyone says they're over, but I don't care. I think they're hot.

• SHOW OFF YOUR NAVEL AND BELLY. I do. Everyone thinks guys are all about boobs and legs. I think they're really into stomachs.

• Dress supersexy when you don't have a boyfriend, or if you want to make your ex-boyfriend jealous. Except you don't want to make him jealous for no reason. Wait till you have a reason. Then go all out.

• To me, anything goes. But that's me. I once wore a tutu with a down parka at the Sundance Film Festival! And stilettos in the snow! The only time anything doesn't go is at the Oscars, where you have to wear something more couture. I'd go with Badgley Mischka, like I did this year, or Valentino. You need to look like a lady at the Oscars. Otherwise, Joan Rivers will tear you apart. Then again, you aren't really anyone till Joan Rivers tears you apart. So wait until you *are* someone, then dress like a lady at the Oscars. I've been on Joan Rivers's worst-dressed list many times, but I don't care what she says.

• The only rule is don't be boring. Dress cute wherever you go. Life is too short to blend in. There are too many cute girls out there not to be making an effort. I don't understand girls who leave the house looking ratty. Are they really that lazy? Or maybe they don't know that punk ended—in the '90s, I think.

How Low Can I Go?

I love low-riding pants. Really low. I hate jeans that go up too high toward your waist; I can't wear them! Brazilian jeans are the best because they're cut so low. I like Frankie B jeans, though they're not quite as low as I like. People tell me they're not trendy anymore, but I've never been one to copy the trends.

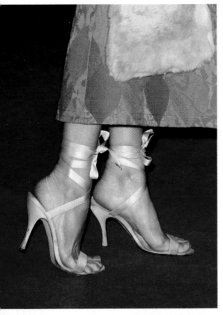

I Love My Stilettos—
the Stairway to Heaven

I love Chanel shoes, Jimmy Choos, Manolo Blahniks, Christian Louboutins, Sergio Rossis, and Gina Londons. To be funky, I'll wear shoes by Hollywould—she's my friend. Sometimes, I'll go to Hollywood Boulevard and buy those cheap high heels—REALLY high. Some of the designers don't make them high enough—although YSL and Gucci do. I love those shoes. It's easy for me to walk in high heels; I've been doing it forever. I can run better in high heels than tennis shoes!

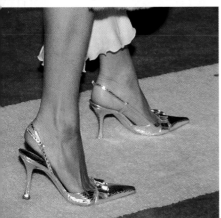

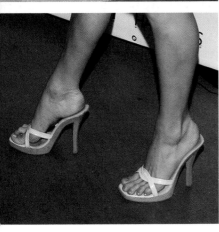

Sweat Suits

They're basically the L.A. uniform, and I like them really, really soft, in cashmere or velour. They should be very feminine, and only in colors like red, pink, or blue. Don't wear boring athletic-gray ones; otherwise, people will think you're working out, and to me, that means you might get sweaty. When I'm home, I always wear cute sweatpants by 2BFree or Juicy Couture. And I'm also working on my very own sweat suit line.

Speaking of which, never talk to guys about going to the gym—they get so bored. They want to think you're naturally gorgeous. I see so many girls telling guys about how much they work out and all the beauty stuff they do. It's boring to talk about that stuff, even with your girlfriends. If I did work out, I would never talk about it, because people should always think you're perfect and it's effortless. After all, you're an heiress.

Fur

Yes, I wear furs for fun, but mostly they're fake. It's important for me to wear as much fake fur as possible, and I like it even more if it *looks* fake. The faker the better! I love animals so much. There are such good fakes out there, I can't understand why anyone would buy a real fur. There's no need to.

Some people might say I'm a hypocrite because I eat burgers but won't wear fur. My response to that is: Heiresses don't need to be consistent.

My Favorite Colors

To me, the only bad colors are red, black, and gray—worn together, they remind me of Freddy Krueger. I love orange. I love purple, though too much purple can make you look like Barney, so you have to watch it. I love yellow. I love blue. I love all colors. And as I've said, I don't like black. Black is boring.

PINK

Pink reminds me of Barbie, who is one of my fashion icons. And pink's so girlie.

I AM CURIOUS IN YELLOW

I love yellow. It's sunny and happy and cheers me up.

MY BLUE PERIOD

My favorite blue is baby blue. It brings out my eyes.

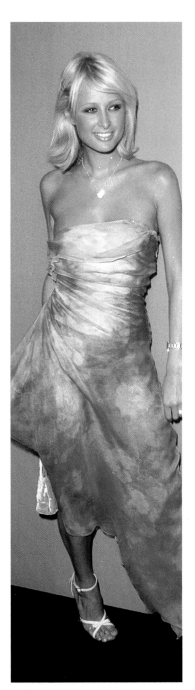

Bad Photos

Yes, it does happen. Even heiresses can take bad pictures—if the lighting's not good or you get distracted. Sometimes I see pictures of myself and I wonder what I was thinking when I wore certain outfits. Sometimes a picture will remind me of a bad day or they'll run a picture of me with my eyes closed. I hate that. Try never to close your eyes when a camera's around. And try to keep certain editors from hating you, although it's inevitable if you're an heiress and, chances are, they're not. (Heiress editors only work at *Town & Country* and *Vogue;* Nicky has done a little guest editing for *Marie Claire*.)

The Evolution of "the Pose"

All these paparazzi guys I've come to know from going out over the years tell me I do a specific kind of pose—and that I've learned to master an entrance. But that makes me embarrassed! I don't really know what I do! I just do it. When I first started being photographed, I just made dumb faces. Then, after looking

over the pictures, I decided to try a few new things. But I'm not going to give away my secrets. Now when I walk into a place everyone goes, "Give us the Paris Pose!" It helps if there's a bunch of cameras flashing. I admire girls who innately know how to do it. If you're going to go down a red carpet, you've got to try to do it right. Do it with attitude. Look at Gwen Stefani—she's awesome.

Just know that if you pose like an heiress, everyone will naturally assume you are one. You don't have to be an actress to have your photo run. Wear the right clothes, turn your hips to the side to slenderize them, and make sure the photographers get all excited when you turn up. Smile sweetly. Next thing you know, your photo will run in *WWD*—and everyone'll just assume you're an heiress. Who's to know the difference? Once you're in the A-list parties, it won't matter anymore.

"If you're going to go down a red carpet, you've got to try to do it right."

Rosa Chá
por Amir Slama

I'm with Paris

Paris

hen I go out, I'm going to be photographed. And part of the reason for that is, I always travel in a pack. Not just any pack, but a pack of really fun girls. I admit it—I do like to walk into a party with my closest friends, but there's nothing spontaneous about it. When I was a little girl, I heard my grandmom telling my mom, "It's better to walk in with a bouquet of roses than be a rose surrounded by a bunch of weeds." I've always liked traveling in packs—it's more fun. If you show up at a party and it's kind of dull, you've brought your own. You know how they say BYOB? I BYOP—bring your own party. If all else fails, you can talk about each other's clothes. It's a no-brainer.

Believe me, it's not easy to arrange a girls' night out for a whole bunch of girly girls. Oh, the burdens of being an heiress! Just making sure they're all dressed and ready at the same time is a nightmare. But I promise you, it's worth it. You get much more attention. Who are guys going to have their heads turned by: one girl—or twenty? Not only that, if you show up with ten or twenty of your girlfriends, you've made sure that a good percentage of the girls in the room are not going to compete with you for guys. If they do, then you've quickly learned they're not your true friends.

Everyone thinks my life is a constant party. It doesn't seem like that to me, but I guess compared to most people, I do go out a lot. Who doesn't want to go out and have fun? If anyone says she doesn't, then she's in denial.

Lately, though, I've been working more, and when I have a boyfriend, I like to stay home. Sometimes.

But when I go out, I want to do it right. After all, I have the rest of my life to stay home—once I hit fifty or so. Just joking! I do want to start a family soon.

My Friends

My closest friends are the girls I grew up with: Nicky, of course, and Nicole Richie, who's been my friend since I was little. Kimberly Stewart, Rod's daughter, and I have known each other since we were two years old, and I love her. And I like the young rocker chicks: Taryn Manning, Fergie from the Black Eyed Peas, Carmen Electra—these girls are so cool. I love Pharrell, he's the hottest record producer out there. I love Matchbox Twenty's Rob Thomas and his wife. They're animal lovers. Jessica Simpson is really cute and really talented; I like her and her husband, Nick, a lot. But the rock chicks I admire most are Gwen Stefani and Madonna. And I have a lot of actress friends, like Dominique Swain and Ashley Scott. Shannon Elizabeth is so sweet and loves animals, like I do. She's into all the animal causes. There's a great, fun, young scene in Hollywood.

I like Alexandra von Furstenberg and her sisters—I really respect and look up to them. I don't hang out with too many socialite girls, except Casey Johnson, a good friend who lives in L.A., and sometimes Amanda Hearst, who's an old family friend. I *love* Naomi Campbell. I've known her for a while and she's one of the most gorgeous women in the world. She always gives me very good advice. And another guy I love in L.A. is Dave Pinsky, from Motorola, because he always gives me free phones.

I'm nice to everyone, because I never want to hurt anyone's feelings. I'll talk to everybody, even if they're boring.

Since the first episode of *The Simple Life* aired, I can't go to a party and not be bombarded by people who want to talk to me. It's not that much fun having people come up to you and want to spend time with you just because they think they should know you. Some of my friends have a name for these hangers-on: "Paris-ites."

My Life Is a Party

The way I look at it, you should live every day as if it were your birthday. So when my birthday comes around, it has to be even more fabulous. For my twenty-first birthday, I had five different parties in five different cities—New York, L.A., Tokyo, London, and Las Vegas—because I have friends in each of those places. So, of course I had to have five different outfits. The traveling didn't bother me; it was worth it to have such a memorable birthday.

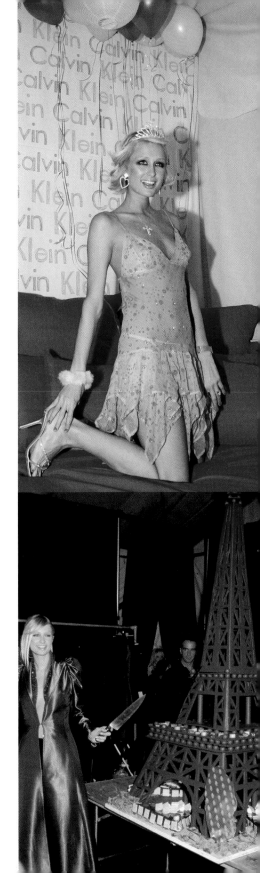

"An entrance

is everything."

My All-time Favorite Places and Parties

• THE IVY ON ROBERTSON IN L.A.: I love the Ivy, which I've been going to ever since I was little. But it's definitely changed over the years. There were a ton of paparazzi outside the last time I went. I LOVE the Ivy's crab cakes—they almost make it worth the mob. It's also a good place to be taken on a date. It means your date is not cheap and he wants to show you off.

• KOI ON LA CIENEGA: It has the best sushi and the cutest crowd.

• CHI ON SUNSET BOULEVARD: It has the best dumplings, and the decor is beautiful.

• MR. CHOW IN NEW YORK AND L.A.: I've been going to these places since I was a little girl. The best food in the world!

• THE PALM IN L.A. AND NEW YORK: I love the lobster and the onion rings. Plus, my picture's painted on the wall, which is pretty cool!

• LE CIRQUE IN NEW YORK: I started going there when I was a baby, and they catered my twenty-first birthday.

• BRENT BOLTHOUSE PARTIES IN L.A.: He's one of the coolest party promoters in town, and everybody's always at his events. The Alliance has cool parties too, which are always exclusive. Exclusive is always better.

• THE *VANITY FAIR* OSCAR PARTY AND THE ELTON JOHN AIDS FOUNDATION OSCAR PARTY COHOSTED BY *INSTYLE:* My favorite. The best-dressed crowd of all time, and everyone is so beautiful. Watching all the gowns and glamour can make you dizzy. I don't need to be around only beautiful people, but it helps: There's a lot more energy; you can feel the sexiness in the air, and that makes everyone excited.

- SUNDANCE FILM FESTIVAL PARTIES: It's all film people, but they're really young and love to stay up late. I love skiing, too. And you can wear jeans and feel dressed up, which is rare for a film festival.

- THE SHORE CLUB AND THE DELANO IN MIAMI.

- LAS VEGAS: For New Year's and for fights, I love to stay at the Palms or any of my family's Vegas casinos, including Caesar's Palace, Bally's, the Flamingo Hilton, the Paris Hilton Casino, and the Vegas Hilton. And I really love the pet stores in Vegas, since they sell exotic animals and ferrets.

My Best-Kept Party Secret

At parties, everyone always thinks I'm drinking—but actually I rarely drink. I live on energy drinks, basically. I LOVE Vitamin Water. I have cases in my house. I drink energy drinks and Vitamin Water all night. That's how I manage to stay up late and never smudge my makeup or mess up my hair. You can see all these girls leaving a party at the end of the night, and they look terrible because they were too out of it to reapply their makeup or even glance in a mirror. This is a huge mistake. People remember how you look when you leave as much as they remember how you looked when you arrived.

But it doesn't bother me when my friends drink. I think it's fun to watch people who are wasted. It's weird, to watch it all. You really read people a lot better. It's funny to watch people and realize how dumb they look. But sometimes, I'm up till five in the morning from all the caffeine I've had. Still, I prefer to be overcaffeinated to being totally out of it. When I get home, I try to drink chamomile tea with milk to fall asleep. I love it with honey or sugar. Both is even better.

Confidence is the Party Key

You've got to walk in like you know everybody there. An entrance is everything. If you walk into a party looking desperate or needy, it's over. Traveling with a pack gives you added confidence—it's like a party-insurance policy.

But stupid stuff can still happen. Recently, I was at a major Hollywood party—everyone was there—and I stepped in a little pond covered by flowers. I didn't see it because of the roses, plus I was on the phone. So I just walked right into the pond. I wasn't embarrassed, just a bit scared. I say that when you're in an embarrassing situation, just laugh at yourself. If you get embarrassed, it will only make the situation worse. So I don't get embarrassed. That's for other people. An heiress should never be embarrassed.

Anyway, nobody can hate someone who's laughing at herself. When I see people in embarrassing situations, I never laugh at them, because I always feel really bad for them. I know how they feel.

"The way I look at it, you should live every day as if it were your birthday."

My
Jet-Set
Life

I've been lucky to have traveled to more fun foreign places during my short lifetime than most people. But it's not so much *where* you go—although that does count, of course—but *how* you get there. What's the good of going to Saint-Tropez or Australia if you're backpacking and you look ratty and act grouchy when you arrive? Or if you can't show up with your hair blown out? Heiresses definitely have a certain way of traveling, and it didn't start with me; it has been documented throughout history. Who do you think bought all that Louis Vuitton luggage, those Hermès dog carriers, fancy steamer trunks, and first-class tickets, not to mention the G5s. If you don't have your own plane, learn how to borrow one, or hitch a ride with your billionaire friends. If you act like you travel that way all the time, chances are you'll get more offers to. Private is so much better. Try to go for the planes with the best chefs. Promise your friends with planes that you'll take them to fun parties and make sure they have a great time when you get to your destination.

And I cannot stress enough the importance of billionaire friends. Even for someone like me, they can be real assets. They raise your social net worth.

How to Pack Like an Heiress

Always pack more than you need—three times as much—then don't wear any of it and buy all new stuff. That's what I do. When they see you coming through the hotel lobby with a ton of luggage, they'll know you're someone important. One of the best ways to explore a new place is to go shopping there. It's always fun to check out shopping bags printed in other languages. I like to collect them. What could tell you more about a culture and its people than their shopping habits?

The only other thing you need to think about when you pack like me is to keep a lot of small cash, in various currencies, around for tips. (You'd never want to haul that luggage around yourself.) If you run out of cash, cast a helpless look

toward the nearest good-looking guy. It never fails. And it helps if you're wearing a short skirt. And high heels.

On Flying

I always try to travel first-class or private.

Forget all that advice about bottled water and sleeping. Here's how I survive really long trips: I love to buy as many gossip magazines as possible, and start the trip by reading everything in the world that's recently been written about me. Then I take a nap, wake up, read scripts, check my e-mail, review personal notes, and write in my diary. It's nice to be in a place where my phone isn't ringing. A plane is pretty much the only place that happens. If I get really bored, I'll pop on my pink mini iPod and reread a *Vogue*. I'll always discover a dress or a pair of shoes I didn't notice before.

I hate the food on planes, so I bring my own fast food, which makes everyone on board mad because it smells so good—and they wish they had it! Sometimes, I'll request a vegetarian meal. They're pretty bland, but they're better than regular plane food. Of course, everybody knows that placing the order does not necessarily mean they'll get it right. That is so annoying. And having a flight attendant spill something on you can totally ruin your flight. It's like, "Hello, I don't want to fly five hours smelling like orange juice."

Slumming It

Yes, I admit I've taken the subway in New York—and it smells. It literally smells like pee. Why can't they do anything about that? Does anyone ever clean down there? And in the summer, you see rats down there, too. Gross. I can deal with ferrets, but rats and sewers, no way. The good thing is, the subway's really fast, which, for a girl on the go, can never be undervalued. I never take the subway in the summertime. But in the winter, I'll do it because it can be the fastest way to get around New York. If I'm not in a rush, I'll usually take a taxi or have a driver in New York. Then again, that's what people expect from me. It really freaks them out if they see me on the subway—and I love that.

MY FAVORITE PLACES

• JAPAN: The people in Tokyo are so sweet, and the kids dress so well. Japan has the best shopping. And I love to go to Nobu there. I also like this club called Lexington Queen. It's where anyone who's anyone in the U.S. can go to hang out while they're in Japan.

• AUSTRALIA: I like Sydney and Melbourne, an Australia's Gold Coast is a lot like Saint-Tropez. I lov Australian accents. They also have the most awesom zoos, where you can hold koalas, play with kanga roos, and swim with dolphins.

MIAMI: The Shore Club and Mansion, the Delano, the Sagamore, Mint and Privé, Opium Bar.

L.A.: Too many great places to mention. That's why I live here.

PALM SPRINGS AND PALM DESERT: I love the weather. It's a great place to relax in the sun.

MALIBU: I love the shopping in Planet Blue at the Cross Creek Mall. They have the best clothes.

EUROPE IN THE SUMMER: Particularly Saint-Tropez, and particularly on a yacht. I love the Byblos Hotel and Les Caves du Roi club, Ibiza, the Mediterranean, and Val Rouge on the beach.

• LAS VEGAS: Totally fun, but it gets old in three days. Never stay more than three days in Vegas. No one cool would.

- LONDON: I love the people, and the shopping is great. I love Harvey Nichols and Harrods—it has absolutely everything!

- BRAZIL: I did a runway modeling job in Rio, and the people were so beautiful. Especially the guys.

- MAUI: I love the Four Seasons there. Hawaii is the best place to get a real tan.

- PARIS: Wasn't it named after me?

- ASPEN: I love skiing, though I am pretty bad at snowboarding (I always fall on my butt). The Little Nell is a great place to stay.

My Least Favorite Places

Anywhere with humid weather. I hate to be anyplace my hair frizzes.

The Hamptons: It's <u>so</u> tired.

The nudist colony where Nicole and I had to stay on <u>The Simple Life 2</u>. Some people should never voluntarily go without clothes.

Maine: I went there once. Good lobster, but there's nothing to do.

Anywhere there's a lot of insects.

Anywhere with bad cell-phone reception.

6

My Day Job

ossibly the best thing about being an heiress is that you don't necessarily have to work. Everyone else must work, though, so it immediately sets you apart. I've never had to have a wardrobe to wear to an office, thank God. I can't imagine anything as boring as wearing some dumb, sexless pantsuit. And since neither Uggs nor stilettos seem to really cut it in an office—unless you work at a Starbucks in Malibu or at *Vogue, Harper's, InStyle,* or *W*—I'd have a tough time. Not only that, I'm not good in the morning. Having to be anywhere before noon seems really uncivilized to me. How are you supposed to have a nightlife if you have to get up before noon?

But how cool is it to be an heiress and decide you *want* to work? It makes you even more special, because there aren't many working heiresses out there, and if they do work, their gigs usually aren't all that glamorous. I know heiresses who've made documentaries about other rich kids, and I'm not even going to comment on those so-called "heiress PR chicks." Would a *real* heiress be out there hawking somebody else's clothing line or party? A real heiress would own the clothing company—and a real heiress doesn't have to do much to get press. All she has to do is show up in the front row of a fashion show and look amazing.

Once I decided to start acting and singing, I think everyone snickered and thought I'd never really pull it off. It's fun proving everyone wrong! And one of the best things is that my parents are really proud of me. Who knew? I found out I like working. It makes you appreciate things more. So, even if people say I'm spoiled, at least they can't say I don't do anything. When they see me at parties now, they know it's probably for a reason. Now I have an agenda like everybody else.

I'm working on a lot of projects, from jewelry, clothing, and handbag design to acting and singing. I've just wrapped up the second season of *The Simple Life,* and I've also had a few fun cameos in movies like *The Cat in the Hat, Wonderland,* and *Raising Helen.* I'm attempting to take the whole acting part of my career to another level. It's so much fun I don't even mind getting up in the morning anymore. Anyway, if all else fails, my bodyguard wakes me up, throws me into the car, and we're on our way. The hair and makeup people do the rest, until I wake up.

Me As Movie Star

Over the summer, I got my first big role in a major studio movie. It's a horror movie called *House of Wax,* and it's a remake of a famous old movie that was made before I was born. Joel Silver produced it for Warner Bros. He also made the *Lethal Weapon* and *Matrix* movies, and I am a huge fan. I love Joel and really appreciate that he believed in me.

We shot on the Gold Coast of Australia this summer with a very cool young cast: Elisha Cuthbert, who's on Fox's *24,* Jared Padalecki, Robert Ri'chard, Brian Van Holt, Jon Abrahams, and Chad Michael Murray, from *One Tree Hill* on the WB.

I was thrilled because I love scary movies, even though they don't really scare me or freak me out; they just make me

> *"I've never had to have a wardrobe to wear to an office, thank God."*

laugh. The only thing I could never do in a movie is be anywhere near insects. Spiders, bugs, daddy longlegs, bumblebees. They really gross me out. But I was fine with all the fake blood and guts, even when they were mine. I had to be fitted for a fake head before we started shooting because, well, you can imagine. I don't want to give too much away.

Acting has become a huge passion of mine, which is why I've done so many TV appearances recently. I've even taken some acting classes, and I really love it. I'll always be perfecting my technique.

Comedies are my favorite. If I could choose any type of movie role, it would be like Cameron Diaz's in *There's Something About Mary*. I also loved the movie *Zoolander*. I like that really sick, silly humor. And making fun of myself is something I've always been good at. Note to the Farrelly brothers, who are always casting funny, ditzy blondes: I'm available. Call my managers. And I'm a big fan of Ben Stiller.

There's no reason I can't do more than one thing. It's all about taking charge and branding yourself. I think we're living in a moment when having a career, especially a really glamorous one, is a very sexy thing. It makes guys want you more, and it makes your whole package a lot more attractive.

My First Album

I started working on this record a while ago. We've cut about six tracks so far, but I keep getting interrupted by acting jobs. I go in the studio and work on it whenever I have time. I hope it comes out in 2004, but I'm not in a rush. It sounds like danceable rock. I LOVE my first single, produced by Robb Boldt, who works with JC Chasez. It's called—and don't take this the wrong way—"Screwed." It's not what you think! It's about a girl who really falls for a guy and knows she's emotionally in too deep and in trouble, so she's screwed. When my parents heard the title, they weren't too happy, but my mother listened to it, and she loves it. When I heard it—before I even recorded it—I didn't even think about the double meaning. But at this point, I'm not afraid of controversy. Everything I do seems to freak somebody out, but I just have to let it go. Some of my friends told me I'm fearless—and that makes me really happy. I like to have fun in almost any form. That is truly what being an heiress is all about. After all, hasn't it been said that having fun is the best revenge?

And it is.

Me As TV Guest Star

This spring, I guest-starred in quite a few TV shows to brush up on my acting skills. I was on *Las Vegas*, playing a girl who's really just in love with money. Trust me, I got the joke. I also shot an episode of *The O.C.* with Mischa Barton and Adam Brody. I played a model-actress who was getting her master's degree in literature. She didn't want her friends to know she was a bookworm.

I also did a guest shot on *George Lopez*. I played his son's tutor. It was my biggest TV role, and we shot for about twelve hours. I had a lot of lines, so for that show, I learned a trick for memorizing them: I find if I write down what I'm supposed to say, I can memorize it.

Me As
Celebrity DJ

Last spring, I was named Best Celebrity DJ at the DanceStar Awards in Miami. I was up against other celebrity DJs, like Adrian Brody, Cameron Douglas, Rosanna Arquette, and Danny Masterson, so it was really exciting to win.

Me As Model

I am currently the face for the Marciano collection and the Guess? line. The campaign was shot by photographer Ellen von Unwerth. I was really thrilled because in the past, they've had great girls like Claudia Schiffer, Drew Barrymore, and Adriana Lima do their magazine ads and billboards—and it was something I always wanted to do. I've also been doing loads of magazine covers and fashion shoots for *Elle, Movieline's Hollywood Life, Seventeen, TV Guide, Rolling Stone,* and *Entertainment Weekly.* Photo shoots take a long time, but I still love the work. It's fun to get paid to have people fuss over you.

I've also learned a lot from working with some of the world's best fashion photographers—people whose work I've been admiring for years. Antoine Verglas really knows how to make a woman look sexy. I love working with David LaChappelle; he's a genius! I love how colorful and creative his photos are. Gilles Bensimon, who shot me in Paris for the March 2004 cover of American *Elle*, was so talented and polite. We shot at the Ritz Hotel in Paris, probably the most beautiful hotel in the world. Paris in Paris. How perfect is that? And Ellen von Unwerth, with whom I just shot the Guess campaign, is incredible. I've always admired the sexiness of her pictures and how alive they are. It is such an honor for me to be the Guess? girl.

I always love working with Jeff Vespa, my favorite photographer. He looks after me, makes sure the best photos of me are the ones that run, and now we've even started doing a bunch of portrait photos together that are very, very pretty.

"It's fun getting paid to have people fuss over you."

The Not-So-Simple Life

I wasn't sure I wanted to do *The Simple Life* when Fox first offered it to me. I hate all the dating reality shows. They are so stupid, and the people on them are so boring. Losers. My mom thought the whole *Simple Life* concept was just trying to make fun of me—a couple of rich girls doing gross jobs on a farm—and I knew she was probably right. At the end of the day, I wound up doing it because I realized it was a TV show meant to be entertainment, and I was just playing a funny role. Anyone who thinks that's really me is in for a total surprise. I thought it would be a fun thing to do with my best friend, Nicole Richie. Not to mention, the producers begged me. Even to an heiress, that's fairly flattering. Particularly to an heiress.

Nicole and I had a great time shooting the show in Arkansas, even though the work was hard. It could have been miserable, but we made the best of it. We brought a lot of cute outfits with us, and coordinated them so we'd flatter each other on camera. But after we left, there was stuff in the tabloids about how everyone in the town hated us. I thought it was interesting, because they loved us when we were there, then called the papers and said bad things about us after we got home. I assume a lot of these people got paid to tell tales. That one boy who had a crush on me apparently got four thousand dollars for every picture he sold of me and him together. I guess I don't really blame him.

On the first installment of *The Simple Life*, Nicole and I

did work every day from six A.M. to five P.M. for minimum wage. I said I never realized people worked hard, but I didn't mean it that way. I know movie producers work hard, and my managers and agents work hard. I guess I didn't realize what hard work meant. Like, dinner at the Ivy in Beverly Hills costs two hundred dollars. Well, I made forty-two dollars a day working, so I'd have to work four or five days just to eat dinner at the Ivy one night! Now that I've worked for that kind of low pay, I understand more what people really go through.

I know a lot of people thought the show was funny, and I love that. Nicole and I might have been naive about farming and stuff like that, but we weren't as naive as they portrayed us on the show. Well, would it have been as funny if we had known what we were doing the whole time? Would it be funny if Jessica Simpson didn't say things about chicken of the sea? People like to laugh at people on reality shows. We get that.

We really *did* do all those gross things. There were no body doubles for that stuff. All the chores were pretty bad, but the thing that grossed me out the absolute worst was when Nicole and I had to go work in a taxidermy place, because I love animals so much. People actually shoot animals to have them displayed dead in their houses! They showed us people who were scraping these bones, and there was all this blood and skin and fat dried up—it was sick. Then we had to scrape the bones with scalpels. They told us the bones were raccoon penises, so we threw them on the floor. Later, Nicole and I thought they were just trying to mess with us. That sucked. But now I think they really *might* have been raccoon penises. Gross!

The Making of The Simple Life 2

The first show was a big hit, so when Fox offered us round two, Nicole and I got to make a few demands. We'd been through a lot, so I knew what to ask for the second time around. I didn't want to have to stay with just one family the whole time, so the second season was set up as a thirty-day cross-country road trip, from Miami Beach to Beverly Hills, with multiple families.

We drove—or, I should say, I drove, because Nicole doesn't have her license—a cotton-candy-pink pickup, and lived in this Airstream trailer that we dragged behind it. It was small and rather gross, and it was so filled up with our and Tinkerbell's outfits that it became a moving closet. There was only one small bed, but we were so tired at night, we'd just pass out from exhaustion. The farthest I'd ever driven before the show was from L.A., to Palm Springs, and that's only two hours. I won't even drive to Vegas from L.A. Driving the trailer was scary because big trucks rocked the Airstream when they passed us. Making turns and backing up were also really hard. I'm amazed we didn't hit anybody. Can you imagine how the press would have dealt with that?

After a while, Nicole and I started to feel sick. I know there were mosquitoes and spi-

ders in that trailer, because we'd wake up with bug bites all over us. There was so much light in there from all the cameras that it attracted every mosquito known to man. And no one cleaned it. And there was no laundry service. Luckily, I never had to wear the same thing more than once, because I brought five million outfits.

We lived on fast food, because in the South, that's all there is (as you know, I love junk food). We weren't allowed to have any money, so we had to beg people to pay for our food, or get the restaurants to give it to us for free. Or if we stayed with a family, they would feed us—but I was usually happier with tacos or fries on the go.

We had to get jobs to make a hundred dollars, which would pay for our gas and food. My first job was at Weeki Wachee, a kids' place with an underwater show. I got to play a mermaid, and Nicole was a turtle. It was kind of stupid, but Elvis had been there, so that made it kind of cool.

For our second job, we stayed with this old guy on his farm somewhere in Florida, and unfortunately, that's where I had a horrible accident with a horse. We had to get on horses to herd bulls into the pen, and we were going really fast. All the cameras were scaring the horses. The boss's horse went really fast, so my horse followed fast. When the cameras started chasing it, my horse started bucking really hard. I went flying into the air and actually fell under the horse. Its hooves went into my stomach and my thigh, and it galloped right on top of me! I was on the ground crying, and the skin on my face and arms puffed up from stinging nettles. They called an ambulance, put an IV in me, and flew me by helicopter to a hospital in Tampa. The IV *really* hurt—I'd never had one before. (And I'm not looking forward to having another one any time soon.) Then they did CAT scans, an MRI, and a lot of tests. Luckily, there was no internal bleeding, just some bruises.

And, of course, the cameras kept shooting till I was off the horse. The press said the reason I was bucked off the horse was because I was wearing high heels. That's so not true! First of all, I was wearing tennis shoes. I know when and where to wear heels, and it's definitely not on a horse. Boy, am I glad that's behind me. I don't know if I'll even be able to watch the show, let alone get on another horse.

After that, I had two days off and stayed in bed. I really needed it. Then Nicole and I went to this crazy nudist resort in Florida. Everyone in the lobby was naked. Even everyone on the street was naked. People were riding bikes wearing shirts and shoes, but no bottoms. That's got to be uncomfortable. Why go bottomless and not topless, I thought? And people accuse *me* of being an exhibitionist! At least we didn't have to get naked in front of them. There was a nightclub in this country club, and when we walked in, we saw all these butt-naked people—fat, naked old people. All the guys wanted to take pictures with us. It was *so* weird. Old ladies, old men, all naked. Even the bartenders. But there was no one cute there, believe me. So what could Nicole and I do? We just started dancing, with our clothes on, to Out-Kast, Britney Spears, "YMCA." Well, it looked like me and Nicole were dancing in a geriatric music video. It was funny, because I'm sure it's the first time in my life I was the person with the most clothes on in the room!

Next, we had to be hotel maids for two days and clean people's rooms. But all we really did was make the beds and put towels away. We weren't going near any dirty laundry. Nicole and I were so lazy, we ended up sitting on a bed, ordering room service, and talking on the phone! Then, like a scene out of *Maid in Manhattan,* Nicole took off her maid's outfit and put on one of the guest's outfits. I put on a towel, and then a real maid came in and did the room, thinking we were the guests. Funny!

After that, I drove twelve hours to Biloxi, Mississippi. And I had to do it, because they shot us driving. There were three cameras on in the car. We stayed with a family who made us eat this gross bacon and build a new pool for them. The son was always yelling at us. Finally, we got so sick of it, we snuck out to a casino. It was not the Bellagio—there were no cute guys anywhere. At least we didn't have to stick around long.

Probably the worst job was having to work in a sausage factory. I never knew sausage was made out of strings of slimy pig intestines. They look like condoms, and you have to push the meat through to make

sausage. I swear, I'll never eat sausage again. Even at the Ivy. Okay, maybe at the Ivy.

After that, we went to a Louisiana swamp and then to Austin, Texas, where we had to work at a concession stand at the baseball game, making French fries. I had no idea they got fried in so much grease! But that isn't going to stop me from eating them. I also had to be a bat-girl, which was kinda fun. I'm not into watching sports, but I like to be around athletic guys. These guys were staring at us so much, they could barely play the game!

The worst part of the second season was begging for money. I admit, I made Nicole do most of the dirty work. Nicole doesn't care—she'll do anything. She's wild and fun. I would just stand there and look cute and smile. I know what I'm good at.

"We really did do all those gross things."

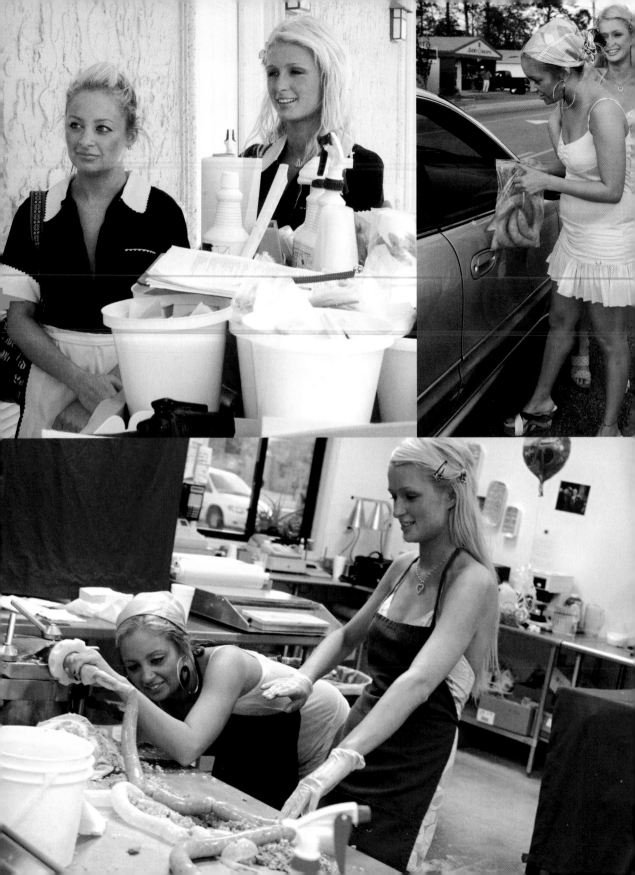

My Best
Accessories

*O*kay, I may be an heiress, and a lot has been handed to me on a platinum platter, but the one place I've had to apply myself, just like every girl, is in studying and analyzing the male species. I may not know how to do brain surgery (who wants to? Guys don't want girls to know that stuff), but I do know the science of what makes a guy tick. I've been told my advice on getting—and keeping—a boyfriend has a very high success rate. When was the last time you saw me without a great-looking boyfriend?

The Kind of Guys I Like

I like guys who are hot, funny, sweet, loyal, honest, and, of course, won't lie or cheat on me. Most important, I want someone who will make me laugh, because I love to laugh. Is that too much to ask? I don't think so. My friends keep telling me I don't prefer one type of guy, and it's true. I admit I like all kinds of guys, just like shoes. But a guy should not be the biggest thing in your life: You should be.

And if you don't believe that, or at least act like it, you will never attract a great guy. You may be dying to have a boyfriend; every girl's been there. Even me. Although, I admit, not for very long. But it shouldn't show. Instead, let your inner heiress come out. Guys do not want girls who are too nice to them, or girls they can walk all over and get too easily. Every guy wants to be with a woman who thinks like an heiress. This is another situation in which being a real one comes in very handy.

The Heiress Way of Flirting

Never be too easy. If you're too easy, a guy knows he has you. Love is a battlefield, right? You may be dying to be with a particular guy, but once he knows it, you've lost almost all your power. If he doesn't need to chase you, he's not going to feel like a real guy. Guys want to compete; it makes them feel important.

I don't ever go up to a guy I don't know—EVER. They should come up to you. You can smile and look cute, but that's all you should do. If you have to do more than that to attract a guy, you aren't *feeling* like you look amazing. Go home and start over.

Don't send your friend up to a guy to bring him over. Then he knows he has you. Girls think that's a subtle move, but it's not. Guys want to be challenged, and they're not as stupid as girls think they are. But they're not as smart, either. An heiress always knows she's the smartest person in the room—at least when it comes to guys. She hasn't had much to

do in life but study guys, so she has the inside track—and the best wardrobe. Not only that: If you don't think guys, even rich ones, are attracted to money, you didn't live through the '90s. It's a whole new world out there. Even guys with a ton of money want to be with women with money. It means they won't have to fight so hard to get a prenup, and that their wedding—if they have one—will be in a good magazine. And their kids are sure to get into the best schools. (Not that I ever cared about that, but people seem to care more and more about that these days.)

So it doesn't hurt to act rich as well as hot. I've found it to be a fairly unbeatable combination. Who's a guy going to go for: a girl who's gorgeous, or a girl who's gorgeous and rich? Borrow your friend's G4—or G5, preferably—and show up in Cannes if he's going to be there. Drop the names of famous hotels that are impossible to book. Read that American Express magazine a couple times, and you'll pick it up. Have good luggage, or very worn crappy luggage: Heiresses could have either. Travel with the right crowd. There are tons of cute girls who started out just hanging with the jet set, which made everyone think they were rich.

It's all about being hard to get. No one would want caviar if it was cheap. People want what they can't have. To attract the guy you want, dress cute but classy—as I have proved! (Okay, sassy works, too.) Hey, it's okay to look really hot some of the time, but

maybe not all the time. Be yourself, be funny, but never, if you like a guy, hit on his friend to make him jealous, or he'll think you're easy. There's a big difference between "hot" and "easy." It's all about how you handle yourself. Be smart, be charming, make him feel important.

How? Look him in the eye when you're talking to him. Act like he's the only guy in the room. Never look away or past him. That's the worst thing you can do, because then he'll know you're searching. Guys don't like that. (I'm not saying don't do it. I'm saying don't get caught.) Compliment him on how he's dressed, mention details like his beautiful eyes, show interest in his life and what he does, ask personal questions. And don't introduce him to your cutest friends until you're sure of him.

On Guys and Your Girlfriends

In most cases, be sure to tell your friends you like a guy *before* they try to date him. Friends who want what you have—those are the ones you don't tell anything to. And you don't always know they're like that till they wake up one day and want something you have. If you're an heiress, it's inevitable. Always keep friends close and enemies closer. Girls can be scandalous when it comes to their friends' boyfriends.

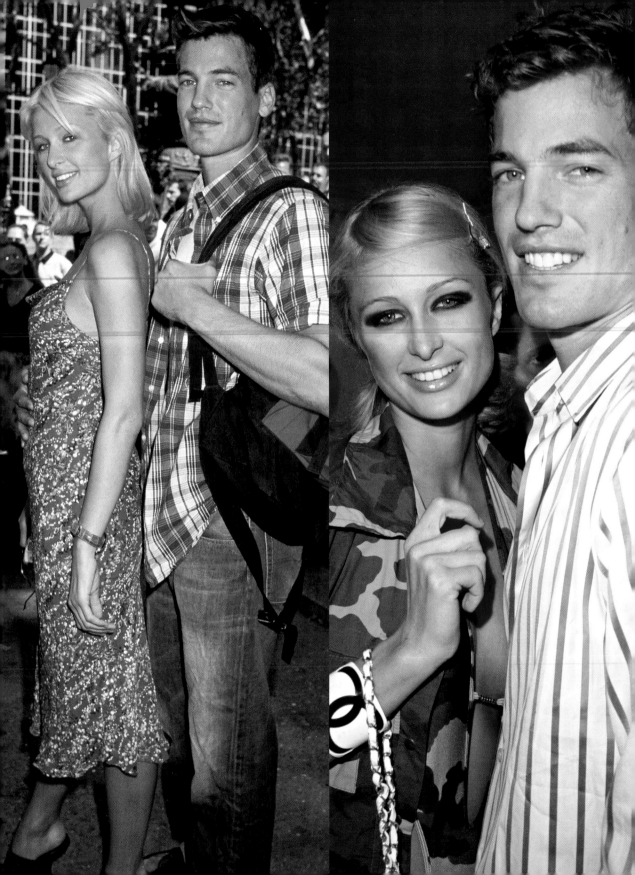

On Getting a Guy to Be Your Boyfriend

Hold out as long as you can. Don't hook up with a guy for a while—until you know he really likes you a lot. If he calls you a lot, then you'll start to know he cares. Try to be as honest as you can because you'll always end up getting caught if you lie. They can tell when you're lying. It's been said that women have a sixth sense, but men have excellent intuition when it comes to girls lying to them. (I've learned my lesson the hard way on that one.) If they think you've lied, chances are they won't trust you again.

How to Know When a Guy's Just After Your Money

An heiress needs to pay attention to these things, since it's inevitable. Does it really matter if a guy's just after your money? Not really, as long as you never give it to him. If you do, he'll probably start cheating on you, spending it on some other girl. All in all, you're better off if the money is a secondary attraction.

If he offers to pay for dinner in the early stages of dating, that's a good sign. Especially in an expensive restaurant. If he talks too much about how you're so rich, and brings up money all the time, I can tell he likes money more than he likes me. I think girls are gold diggers more often than guys

though. I haven't met too many guys who were out for my money. I think when it comes to girls, guys are motivated more by attraction than by money. At least at my age. And it helps if you like famous guys, because they usually have their own money. Who's George Clooney dating now?

When to Kick Him to the Curb

A lot of girls are bad at dumping guys. I'm not one of them. Heiresses have to be brazen about these things. It's a fact of life. If you've never dumped a guy, no guy is really going to respect you or be afraid of you. You need to let your boyfriend know that if he makes a wrong move, he'll be tossed out in a heartbeat. It keeps him on his toes, and that's exactly where you want him. At all times.

What constitutes a wrong move? If he lies to you or cheats on you. No exceptions. I know everybody, so I can always find out what a guy's up to. Everyone calls and tells me everything—guys wouldn't risk lying to or cheating on me. Being so connected that no one can mess with you is a good heiress strategy. Somebody you know is going to know someone else—even in Europe or Japan—you can get info from. I make friends with my boyfriends' bodyguards. I get their cellphone numbers. I have spies everywhere. Heiresses always have networks.

And most important to remember: If a guy cheated with you on his girlfriend, he'll do it to you too. If he won't touch you till he breaks up with a girl he's with but kind of over, that's a good sign. A lot of my friends will keep a cheating guy around because they don't want to be alone—don't do that!

You'll always get your heart broken. A true heiress never gets her heart broken. She is the one breaking hearts. And it's never a bad idea to have another guy waiting in the wings, just in case. Always have a list of good backup guys in your head, and when you spot one of them—even if you're with your boyfriend—smile at him with the look of "Who knows? You could be next." He'll get it.

Just don't get caught. And if you do, deny it. Heiresses are very good liars when they have to be.

Straightening Out Old Rumors

If you believe the papers, I've been linked with everyone from Eddie Furlong to Nicolas Cage. Where do they come up with these things? There doesn't seem to be a guy on earth—at least a famous guy—they think I haven't dated. I was even accused of breaking up the marriage of movie producer Robert Evans. How ridiculous is that? When I heard that one, I had heard everything. Come on! I was twenty-two when his marriage broke up. He's seventy-three!! He's a little old for me! The rumors about me and Mark McGrath were complete lies, too. We were both laughing about that, wondering where it came from. Mark's my friend.

Contrary to everything you might think, I really prefer having one boyfriend. I'm friends with a lot of guys, but I don't like dating unless I'm *really* into somebody.

I tend to fall for guys who are cool. One thing that always attracts me: guys who sing. I think a guy who can sing is really sexy. Singing is the hardest thing to do because it's so easy to get embarrassed—singing takes confidence. Plus, he can write

songs about me. I admit I'm also attracted to pretty-boy male models. They're not always so smart, but they are hot.

Here's something only an heiress would do: Once you break up with a guy, it's a good idea to torture him—*if* you're bored. Men have treated women badly throughout the ages; they never seem to take them seriously. So why shouldn't we have a little fun at their expense? If you're really feeling your inner heiress, you will never let a guy get the best of you. And, God forbid, if you do, *never show it.* If you torture them, they'll have a much worse time getting over you. And that's what you want. An heiress has to be memorable.

"When was the last time you saw me without a great-looking boyfriend?"

My
Fashion
Don'ts

*Y*ou know those *Glamour* Don'ts? The things you shouldn't wear because everyone everywhere is supposed to know they're in bad taste? Well, I've worn a lot of them! With clothes, I've never really drawn the line between "good taste" and "bad taste." I mean, where would all these pop stars be if they followed that advice? Or John Galliano, for that matter? Who's to say what's good taste or bad—some boring old socialites in New York? Why on earth would I want to listen to *them*? Do they have cute guys around them all the time, or do I?

"Who's to say what's good taste or bad— some boring old socialites in New York?"

THE DON'TS
ACCORDING TO ME

I call this pose the "Y" pose, because of the shape my arms are making. I should call it the "Why?" pose, because it looks so dumb!

PLAYSTATION 2 PARTY ↑

Don't ever pose like that! That pose has got to go! Don't wear sunglasses at night. And forget black shoes with a white dress. I should have worn silver shoes. And those cuff bracelets—what was I thinking? I used to wear two at all times. I'm so over it.

I packed for L.A. and didn't realize I was going to Sundance. I look like Army Barbie in that Pucci dress—and the shoes are just awful. But I thought this looked cute at the time.

SUNDANCE FILM FESTIVAL ↑
Okay, I've now learned the hard way not to use props in photos. I was attempting to do karaoke with a water bottle, and I don't think it came off well. And I'm sure I never wore that Hugo Boss glow-in-the-dark parka again.

↗ *This was a fancy diamond dog collar—but now that I look at it, it looks more appropriate for whiplash than a party.*

↖ *I do love those jeans. That's a top you can tie any which way. I thought it looked hot, but now I think it looks a bit like a rubber band.*

↖ Vegas Showgirl Barbie! But, hey, it was my birthday!!! Trust me—nobody ignored me that night!

↗ Okay, Deadhead Barbie. Or is it Hippie Granola Barbie? I look like an old lady! Did that dress belong to Jerry Garcia in another life? This is the worst outfit I've worn— EVER!

This is just pink overload! At least I match the backdrop! But I guess there is such a thing as being too tan.

↗ I didn't want to wear this hat, but I had to—it was for Philip Treacy's party, and he's a famous hat designer. I didn't want to disappoint him. But I love Boy George; he's wackier than me! And he dresses even more outrageously than I do.

↗ Okay, *what a shirt not to wear! It was for the premiere of the movie* Blow, *and we just weren't thinking people would automatically think that. It gives people the wrong idea.*

↗ *I was doing a photo shoot and went right to the Movieline Awards. I think everyone thought I was trying to be Pris from Blade Runner.*

↗ *It's bad to mix two different camo-prints together. Plus I'm wearing a bikini top to a party at night! Oh, well. Won't make that mistake again.*

I'm thinking I'm a Barbie in this picture. I did feel a little bit like a princess that night. But now that I look at it, I look more like Courtney Love Barbie!

I like wearing push-up bras—it's fun to pretend you have boobs once in a while. But the annoying part is that everyone wrote that I had my boobs done!

Warm and Fuzzy

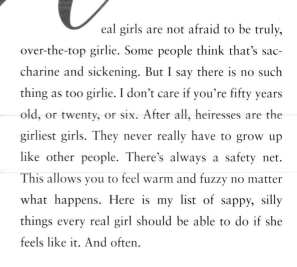

*R*eal girls are not afraid to be truly, over-the-top girlie. Some people think that's saccharine and sickening. But I say there is no such thing as too girlie. I don't care if you're fifty years old, or twenty, or six. After all, heiresses are the girliest girls. They never really have to grow up like other people. There's always a safety net. This allows you to feel warm and fuzzy no matter what happens. Here is my list of sappy, silly things every real girl should be able to do if she feels like it. And often.

• Throw a fit, throw things, cry—loud. Have a meltdown whenever you feel like it. Whimper and whine on a whim.
• Change your mood like you change your clothes. Or even more often.
• Change your boyfriend as often as your mood.
• Let your parents take care of you.
• Wear pink and ballerina stuff to the point of overkill.
• Keep stuffed animals all over your room, and carry them wherever.
• Talk on the phone wherever and whenever you feel like it.
• Cover your cell phone in rhinestones.
• Keep a diary of everything a guy you like does.

But what makes me feel the warmest and fuzziest is my family—and my dog, Tinkerbell. Let's start with my human family.

As I said earlier, it's okay to make up your lineage—so many heiresses have—but you've got to keep the story straight. Luckily, I don't have to do that. My lineage is real. Everyone knows the story of my family; it's been written about so many times. Conrad Hilton was my great-grandfather, and he started this huge hotel empire. He was pretty famous for a lot of things, including being married to Zsa Zsa Gabor. My grandfather, named Conrad Hilton, was called Nicky and was the first of Elizabeth Taylor's seven husbands. (Another good heir or heiress rule of thumb: If you have to be one of a group, it's best to be first.)

It's traditional for an heiress to be raised in an insular way. No one thinks that's true of me, but actually it was. When I was growing up, my parents were very strict, especially my mother. We were brought up to be very humble. The rumor is that I got a credit card at age nine, which is ridiculous. It was more like nineteen, and I had to get one myself without my parents. We had rules and regulations. Even when Nicky and I started going out as teenagers in New York, our parents kept a close eye on us. We had to check in with them like ten times a day. I had a curfew of midnight until I was seventeen. People think my parents let us do whatever we wanted, but that wasn't true at all, trust me. I got punished as much as anyone.

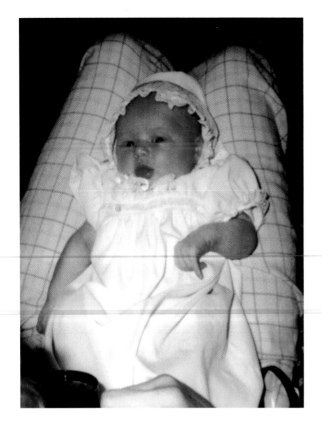

Mom and Dad

My dad, Rick, was the support system in the house. He videotaped everything the kids did—my birth, my sister's and brothers', and all of my cousins' births! He got us through every crisis. Even though I'm the oldest, I admit, I *am* still daddy's little girl. This is exactly what an heiress is supposed to be. My dad, Rick, supports me in everything I do.

My mom's the best, and she's been there for me through everything. I'm always proud to walk into a room with her. After all, doesn't everyone say guys check out your mom to see how you'll turn out? In my case, I'm very happy to show off my mom. She's drop-dead gorgeous.

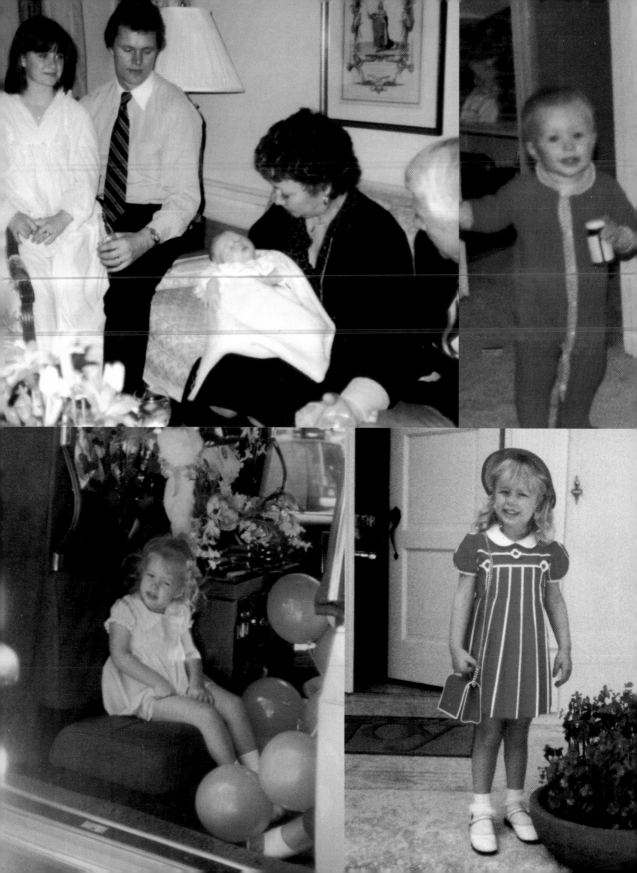

What's great is my parents are still really young and cool. And it's cool they're together, not divorced. They've been together since my mom was fifteen. She was nineteen when she had me, so she's almost like an older sister. My dad is an animal lover, like me. He took me to exotic pet shows when I was a kid, and he bought me whatever animal I wanted. That led to my lifelong love of animals. My parents still have a ton of dogs and cats at their house in the Hamptons.

Childhood Memories

My family is pretty huge, and I've always loved that. My mom has two sisters, Kyle and Kim Richards (both actresses), who were really young when I was born. They both live in L.A. and are almost like older sisters. My dad has five brothers and two sisters. And they all have kids! On my mom's side alone, I have ten cousins. They all grew up in L.A., so the holidays were really fun when we were kids. Christmas time was really wild in our house. I think my mom thought she was Mrs. Claus. She'd start decorating for Christmas right after Halloween. There was, like, a tree in every room. And when Santa came to our house, he was a Beverly Hills Santa, in a red Mercedes!

Every Easter—even now—my parents would make the best Easter-egg hunt. There were eggs everywhere. A lot of the plastic eggs had money in them, so none of us would even bother to pick up the hard-boiled ones! What's the point? The best part was that my parents would buy little yellow chicks, baby ducks, and bunnies for us. I'd keep the chicks till they turned into roosters—

then they'd grow these gross red things on their heads and under their beaks, and they'd cock-a-doodle-do every morning at dawn. Our neighbors in Bel Air didn't really appreciate that. So I would have to give them away.

As kids, we would spend time at my grandfather Barron Hilton's different houses. Sometimes, my family would take Nicky and me to the Duck Club in Northern California, where the men would hunt ducks. Nicky and I would collect frogs. I remember I had a pet ferret I named Farrah the Ferret, after my cousin Farrah Richards. We would also spend a lot of time at my grandfather's Bel Air house, called Brooklawn.

Tinkerbell

I got Tinkerbell one Halloween, and we're pretty inseparable. She's a tiny, two-pound teacup Chihuahua, one of the smallest of her breed in the world, and a "deerhead" as opposed to an "applehead." I'm not totally sure what that means, but I think it means that she looks more like a deer than an alien. I got her online, from a breeder at TexasTeacups.com. She arrived on a plane, which was very fitting for an heiress's dog. She's a little princess, so cute and sweet. A little lady. I call her Tink for short. Of course, some people think this is impossibly girlie. For me, it's just normal. If I had to have a larger dog, I would be completely grossed out. Plus, Tink is entirely portable.

Tink doesn't even like other dogs—she acts just like a human! I know Tink and I are a lot alike, and Tink thinks a lot like me. I mean, she eats like me—she loves fast food and steaks. But obviously, her stomach is a lot smaller. I'm her stylist, and I can tell you she dresses really cute! She wears a lot of Fifi & Romeo coats in pink and white, and some have

little cherries on them. And she also has really cute shoes. A lot of designers who've
seen us in pictures together send me cute outfits for her. But I want to create a line of
doggy clothes called Paris and Tinkerbell.
She's the best dog in the world: She can get
really excited, but she can still chill. I take her
everywhere with me. She sits on my lap on
planes, and no one minds because she's so
cute. Everyone loves Tink.

Besides teacup Chihuahuas, I've got a
thing for other very small, cute animals, like
ducks, guinea pigs, and ferrets. Last spring, I
was in Vegas, and I got two ferrets, a boy and
a girl. You have to buy them there because
it's one of the few places where it's legal to
sell them. I always go to the pet stores in Vegas. Now these ferrets frolic with Tink on the
floor of my house, and they climb all over
each other. It's really fun to watch. Every so
often, they get lost under the couch, but I've
actually learned how to discipline them. Now
I'm going to get the ferrets little outfits, too.
They're so small, they can't even wear Tink's
hand-me-downs.

I was imagining what it would be like if
Tink kept a diary. How fun would that be! So
we got together and I helped her write it;
now you and your pets can have a peek at the
life of an heiress's dog.

TINKERBELL HILTON'S DOGGY DIARY

A BRIEF EXCERPT

by Tinkerbell Hilton

Today it was nice out, and Paris took me for a walk in the Hollywood Hills. Afterward, her driver took us to the dog park, because Paris thought there might be cute guys there. But I refused to play with any of the mutts that were running around. I really only like to hang out with poodles. The really small, fluffy ones.

That's because, if I may say so myself, I have excellent breeding and manners. I never pee on the floor. Okay, maybe sometimes, when Paris forgets to take me out enough. But I always attempt to pee outside. If I do pee inside, there's always somebody around to wipe it up fast enough so that no one really knows it was me. They think I'm even better trained than I am.

I also have excellent grooming, and those mutts at the dog park can see that from a mile away. They were all over me today—literally! I don't really blame them, though. I have my nails painted pink to go with my many cute coats. I'm wearing one of my adorable Fifi & Romeo coats. (I also have cute shoes to wear, if Paris wants to really dress me up.) I never go anywhere without my Swarovski crystal–covered leash. Of course, an heiress's dog such as myself doesn't really need a leash; I only have one because it looks good and goes with my coloring. I'm smart enough to never run away—I know I have a good thing going here! I get to eat steak and hamburgers, and even Häagen-Dazs, if I'm really good or if Paris has the late-night munchies. Really, you know, I'm more human than pup—or I'm smart enough to act that way, because that's what people expect from an heiress's dog. And truly, I do like people better than dogs, because every dog is ten times my size—and scares the crap out of me! Whoops! I mean the *be-jesus*!!! I try never to swear, even when I'm barking mad. A well-bred dog does not swear, even when she's barking or growling.

After we got home from the dog park, Paris started surfing the Internet and found another website that has teacup Chihuahuas. She wants to get a boy dog to keep me company. She thinks I should have a boyfriend. She wants to name him Peter Pan. But she can't seem to find another teacup as small as me. Let's face it, most other Chihuahuas look like cows compared to me! So I'm not worried that I'll get a little male Chihuahua I have to compete with for food or clothes. First of all, he'd probably be gay, in which case he'd leave me alone. Or else she'll get sick of him and give him away to some boyfriend she's ready to get rid of. And then I'll have her all to myself again. And that's just the way I want to keep it. After all, I'm an heiress's dog. I know how to be a diva.

Personal Space

I know people don't think of me as a girl with a lot of downtime. But you can't look like I do at events if you never take time for yourself. And you can't really be on at parties and know as many people as I do without retreating once in a while.

This aspect of my life is a very intentional mystery to most. Remember what I said about keeping some things mysterious? But I'm sure you've often found yourself wondering, What does Paris do behind closed doors? Finally, I'm going to give you a little peek at my private life.

Yes, I do have one.

First of all, I love to cook. It's so much fun to be able to make yourself a great meal. And Nicky and I both love to bake. A lot of times, I'll cook at home for friends and we'll watch movies. I'm particularly good at pasta, and I always cook for my boyfriends. The good news about being an heiress-cook is, I don't have to clean up. If I did, I'd probably never do it. Really, I don't know how housewives do it. If you cooked *and* cleaned—and, God forbid, had a job, too—you'd never have time for yourself. Or a decent social life.

Every so often, when I feel like I have to get out of L.A., I go to Palm Springs—we have a couple of houses there—or the San Diego Hilton, where my cousins live. For the most part, these places are so boring that I get my adrenaline back within a few days, and then I'm out of there. I'm always longing for a city, and shopping, and civilized things. But doing spa treatments in places like Palm Springs forces you to calm down, and it's really fun to be pampered.

But my favorite thing to do to relax, at home or on vacation, is to take a delicious bath with very girlie products. I take more baths than showers. Or, to get really super clean, I take a shower first, then a bath. I love Acqua di Parma products, but Caresse smells good, too, even though you can buy it at Rite Aid. It might be cheap, but I love it—it smells so good. There really are no bad bath products. And a girl cannot have too many. I really like this body stuff called Butter Crème Doo Wop—it smells like icing. And I love Chanel bath products. And products from the Body Shop. I'm telling you, you don't have to use only expensive stuff. The cheap stuff's good too, if it smells nice. Guys can't tell the difference.

I like classical music to relax to. I remember when I was little, my mom would put the classical channel on the radio for us to fall asleep to. There's nothing as feminine or calming as a long bubble bath in a beautiful pink bathroom with great music. It makes me feel like Marilyn Monroe or Jayne Mansfield. And whenever you see an heiress in a movie, isn't she in some beautiful bubble bath, with a feathery robe and slippers waiting next to it?

It doesn't matter if you don't have a giant bathtub like I do, or a pink robe to climb into. There are other very girlie indulgences you can have that make life seem a little sweeter. Here are some of mine:

My Favorite Music

Madonna may be my favorite—and obviously, I've learned a lot from her. I've loved her as long as I can remember; she's my idol. I also love Blondie (but I would, wouldn't I?). Debbie Harry rules. The other music I play when I'm home or driving is Pink, Matchbox Twenty, OutKast, the Neptunes, Justin Timberlake, 50 Cent, the Black Eyed Peas, Cyndi Lauper, and anything by my Japanese friend Yoshiki.

My Favorite Books

Contrary to what people think, I do read a lot. I love Candace Bushnell's *Sex and the City* and *Four Blondes, Maneater* by Gigi Levangie Grazer, Plum Sykes's *Bergdorf Blondes, The Great Gatsby* by F. Scott Fitzgerald, Betina Zikha's *Ultimate Style: the Best of the Best-Dressed List*, and anything by Jackie Collins.

My Favorite Magazines

I always read *Us Weekly, In Touch, People, Vogue, Lucky, Harper's Bazaar, Elle, Vanity Fair, GQ, Rolling Stone, Entertainment Weekly, InStyle, Teen People, Cosmo, Blender, and FHM.* Also, the Abercrombie & Fitch catalog has very cute guys in it.

The Next Chapter

_P_eople always ask me what I think I'll be like when I'm older. I've pretty much grown up in public, and I've done some pretty immature things along the way, but this is the fate of every heiress. Everyone does crazy stuff when they're young, but if you're an heiress, you have even more opportunities to mess up. And everything tends to get written about, so people don't forget as easily. I learned this lesson the hard way. Now I know that everyone's had embarrassing moments, but we don't really hear about them if they're not famous, because no one really cares.

I've definitely gotten a lot more serious in the last couple of years. I'm going to keep acting and writing music, and hopefully I'll be able to follow this album with another. I'm quite serious about the music thing. I love it. And work tends to keep me out of trouble. I barely have time to get in trouble anymore.

Along with the Heiress line of jewelry I've been working on, I've also been developing a line of clothes. But I would make sure everyone could afford it, because I think everyone should be able to dress like an heiress. Dressing up and defining my sense of style, no matter what anybody else thinks of it, has given me a lot of confidence, and I'd like to pass that on to younger girls. There are just too many boring black dresses out there right now, and it's not fair. Not everyone can afford Dolce & Gabbana and Roberto Cavalli, but they'll be able to buy my clothes and look really hot.

But believe it or not, I don't always want the glamorous, jet-set life. Let's face it, I've done it. The ones who are in their thirties and forties and do it now were high school nerds.

That wasn't me. Someday soon, I want to have children and a big house with a lot of animals—like my parents had. I would like to be a young mom, like my mom was. My parents have been together forever, and I'd like to follow their good example. I mean, look how I turned out!

On Moving Forward

I've been through a lot in the last few years, a lot of ups and downs, and it's all been an incredible learning experience for me. I turned twenty-three on February 27, 2004, but the last year has been so intense, I know it was my biggest leap in terms of growing and changing. I've always felt so young, but suddenly I feel much more adult. I never thought I'd be proud of that! I will always be me, Paris, and I will probably always love to have fun, dress up, and go out and shine. Self-reflection was never my strong point when I was younger, and I was okay with that. But I really learned who is always there for me, supporting me: my parents, my sister and brothers, and the rest of my family who love me through the good and the bad.

I have a much deeper appreciation of them, their strength, and also, my strength. I've learned you don't grow that much when things are good; you really grow in the tough times. When you get hurt, life gets very real, and then you have to stop and put the world in focus. I'm glad I was forced to do that this year. There's been a huge shift in my self-perception and the way I look at the world. I know more than ever how lucky I am, how blessed I've been, and as a result, I think I got a lot more serious. What you've just read and seen is a slice of me becoming me: an heiress, yes, fun-loving and, I admit, privileged, and even pretty worldly for twenty-three.

But now I can feel myself becoming a grown-up with real goals. Sure, it's been great having so much attention. Who wouldn't want that? But now I want attention not just for being Paris, but for what Paris, the professional, has accomplished: a TV career, a modeling career, a book, a start in music, and the knowledge that anything you try, you can absolutely pull off, no matter what anyone writes or says about you. That only gave me more to prove. And you can have just as much fun when you work as when you play. Getting photographed and getting treated like a star is fun. But having a dream and actually making it happen is so much more thrilling. Now I know I really can do anything I want. And that's what being an heiress is all about.

And I'd say I've proved that, haven't I? And I'm only just getting started. . . .

STYLE CREDITS

All chapter opening photographs and cover photograph by Jeff Vespa

Produced by Andrea Collins
Makeup by Geoffrey Rodriguez • Hair by Julio Hernandez • Styling by Victor Alegria
Prop styling by Edward Murphy

FRONT COVER
Dress by BCBG • Jewelry by Chopard • Shoes by Jimmy Choo

CHAPTER ONE
Dress by Elie Saab • Jewelry by Doris Panos • Sheets by Frette

CHAPTER TWO
Nicki's dress by BCBG • Paris's dress by Matthew Williamson • Shoes by Sergio Rossi

CHAPTER THREE
Jeans by Blue Cult • Shoes by Paolo

CHAPTER FIVE
Pamela Roland skirt • Jewelry by Nancy Davis Peace & Love Collection

CHAPTER SIX
Suit by Chanel • Shoes by Chanel

CHAPTER SEVEN
Halter top available at Palace Costumes • Jean shorts by GUESS?

CHAPTER EIGHT
Dress by Douglas Hannant • Jewelry by Chopard • Pink watch by Chronotech

CHAPTER TEN
Top and skirt by Chanel

CHAPTER ELEVEN
Diamond earrings by Doris Panos

CHAPTER TWELVE
Cashmere scarf by Juniper & Jasper • Sweat suit by Juicy Couture
Mercedes-Benz SL600 courtesy of Mercedes-Benz USA, LLC

All photos provided by WireImage and its photographers unless otherwise noted.

Courtesy of Nicky Hilton; Donato Sardella; Michael Caulfield • Page 80: Jeff Vespa • Page 81: *(Clockwise from left)* Jeff Vespa; Seth Browarnik; Denise Truscello • Page 82: Jeff Vespa; Denise Truscello • Page 83: *(Clockwise from left)* Jeff Klein; Jeff Vespa; Ron Galella • Page 84: Theo Wargo; Chris Weeks • Page 85: *(Clockwise from top left)* Jeff Vespa; Jemal Countess; Denise Truscello • Page 86: Jeff Vespa

CHAPTER FIVE

Page 89: Jeff Vespa • Page 90: Courtesy of Jason Moore • Page 91: Courtesy of Nicky Hilton • Page 92: Courtesy of Jason Moore • Page 93–95: Courtesy of Nicky Hilton (11) • Page 96: *(Clockwise from top right)* Queen; Courtesy of Nicky Hilton (3)

CHAPTER SIX

Pages 99–103: Jeff Vespa (4) • Page 104: Jeff Vespa (2); *George Lopez* photo, Justin Lubin/Warner Bros. TV, © 2004 Warner Bros. Entertainment Inc., All Rights Reserved • Page 105: Jeff Vespa; cover image courtesy of *Seventeen* magazine, photograph by George Holz • Page 106: Jeff Vespa; Jesse Grant • Pages 107–109: Jesse Grant (6)

CHAPTER SEVEN

Page 111: Jeff Vespa • Page 112: Sam Jones/FOX • Pages 113–115: Michael Yarish/FOX (3) • Pages 116–118: Jeff Vespa (4) • Page 119: Sam Jones/FOX • Page 120: Ray Mickshaw (2) • Page 121: Michael Yarish/FOX • Page 122: Jeff Vespa • Page 123: Ray Mickshaw (2) • Page 124: Michael Yarish/FOX (2) • Page 125: Jeff Vespa • Page 126: Michael Yarish/FOX (3) • Page 127: Ray Mickshaw; Michael Yarish/FOX

CHAPTER EIGHT

Pages 129–131: Jeff Vespa (3) • Page 132: Jeffrey Mayer • Page 133: George Pimentel; Jean-Paul Aussenard • Page 135: *(Clockwise from top left)* Rodrigo Varela; Donato Sardella; Jeff Vespa; Lester Cohen • Page 136: Carmen Valdes; Jeff Vespa • Page 137: Dimitrios Kambouris • Page 138: Steve Jennings • Page 139: Jeff Klein • Page 140: Larry Busacca; Michael Caulfield • Page 141: Jeff Vespa

CHAPTER NINE

Page 143: Jeff Vespa • Page 145: Steve Granitz; Sam Levi • Page 146: Jeff Vespa; Doug Piburn • Page 147: Theo Wargo; Jim Spellman • Page 148: Jeff Vespa (2) • Page 149: Alan Davidson; Steve Granitz • Page 150: *(Clockwise from top left)* Jean-Paul Aussenard; Jeff Vespa (2) • Page 151: Jeff Vespa • Page 152: Theo Wargo; Jean-Paul Aussenard • Page 153: Steve Granitz; Mike Guastella

CHAPTER TEN

Pages 155–156: Jeff Vespa (2) • Page 157: Courtesy of Cathy Hilton; Carmen Valdes • Page 158: Courtesy of Kyle Richards (2) • Page 159: Courtesy of Kyle Richards (2); Ray Mickshaw • Pages 160–161: Courtesy of Kyle Richards (8) • Page 162: Courtesy of Kyle Richards; Ray Mickshaw • Page 163: Jeff Vespa • Page 164: Courtesy of Kyle Richards (3) • Page 165: Courtesy of Kyle Richards (2), *(bottom right)* Jeff Vespa • Page 167: Jeff Vespa • Page 168: Jesse Grant

CHAPTER ELEVEN
Page 171: Jeff Vespa

CHAPTER TWELVE
Page 175: Jeff Vespa • Page 179: Courtesy of Cathy Richards (5)

ENDPAPERS
Jeff Vespa; courtesy of Nicky Hilton; courtesy of Kyle Richards; Kevin Mazur; Jesse Grant; Chris Weeks

Best Wishes for the Holidays
and for
Peace, Health and Happiness
throughout the New Year

The Hilton Family
Kathy, Rick, Paris, Nicky, Barron, Conrad
Dolce, Sebastien and Tinkerbell too